The Odyssey Trail

From Dreams to Doing—
Footprints Across the World

A collection of columns from *The Review*

Belden & Lisa Paulson

In Dialogue with Barry Johanson,
Publisher of *The Review* in Plymouth, Wisconsin

Thistlefield Books
Plymouth, Wisconsin

The Odyssey Trail: From Dreams to Doing—Footprints Across the World

A collection of columns from *The Review*

by Belden & Lisa Paulson

ISBN-13: 978-0-9816906-7-4

Library of Congress Control Number: 2018940045

Design and Production: Kate Hawley by Design

Proofreader: Paula Haubrich

Thistlefield Books

W7122 County Road U

Plymouth, Wisconsin 53073

(920)528-8488 • www.ThistlefieldBooks.com

For the readers of *The Review*,
and all those who are up for
imagining and creating
a better future

Table of Contents

INTRODUCTION

It was a warm summer afternoon in 1980. Barry Johanson, the young editor-publisher of *The Review,* the distinguished small-town Plymouth newspaper, had come with Christie, his wife and collaborator, to chat in the backyard of our old farmhouse. They were curious about a rumor that the couple who had bought the William Miller farm in the town of Mitchell was contemplating creating there an "Eco School: Education for Living in a Time of Transformation." What was that about?

Lisa had sketched out a rather fanciful dream for an experiment that might model "the good life," where people could come to live in harmonious cooperation with nature and each other. Hesitantly, she showed this to Barry. To our astonishment, the following week he printed it in this twice-weekly community newspaper dating back to 1895.

So began a long, friendly connection where Barry followed our out-of-the-box ideas and adventures that were taking us around the world. He heard how we'd met in the slums of Italy helping bombed-out Neapolitans and Eastern European refugees after World War II. How in 1968 Bel had been accused of being a CIA spy when he went to research political obstacles to economic development in Northeast Brazil (and where Lisa was zapped by a voodoo evil eye spell). And when we'd found ourselves in

Tiananmen Square in 1989 on the eve of the Chinese uprising there.

Eight years ago Barry, came to us with a proposition. He had just read Bel's 2009 book, *Odyssey of a Practical Visionary,* and thought his readers would be interested in a dialogue—where he would ask questions of both of us about events discussed in that book, and we would respond. For the column called "Odyssey," most of the articles appear under Bel's name; some are under Lisa's, and a few have input from both of us.

Barry's questions ranged over issues that the nation and the world were currently dealing with, both at the time the articles were being written, and from earlier eras Bel's book described when we ourselves were heavily involved in addressing some of those challenges.

Since writing the columns, new issues have arisen or become more acute: the proliferation of dangerous drugs; the diminution or eradication of jobs young people starting out had always depended on; an awareness of extreme climate conditions and multiplying natural disasters that has moved front and center.

A good chunk of our energy over the last thirty years has gone into envisioning and creating equitable, sustainable communities. We see an even greater need now—and often a thirst—for living configurations that are interconnected and based on mutual interdependence and caring.

Besides looking at the obvious challenges we and the world are facing, we hope you'll enjoy getting to know your Sheboygan County neighbors a bit better—our family, our explorations and escapades in this country and abroad.

We hope that bringing the collection of columns that were spread out over a year into one concise volume will provide an interesting retrospective, not only of the lives of two Plymouth (Mitchell) residents, but of times past and present, which may inspire others to share their own adventures.

Belden and Lisa Paulson

January 19, 2010

Introducing ODYSSEY

by Barry Johanson, publisher of *The Review*

THE COLUMN "**Odyssey**" by Belden Paulson is an interview format that I originated around the theme of creating a better world. I ask Paulson, who has a unique and innovative association with Plymouth and central Sheboygan County, a question drawn from what started as a letter to his four grandchildren (Lark, Niko, Katie, and Nicky). The kernel of that letter heated up for several years in a cooker fanned by his family and friends until it finally blew up like popcorn into a 757-page book—www.thistlefieldbooks.com—a family publishing enterprise.

Imagine the kids getting *Odyssey of a Practical Visionary: Eco-Communities • Sustainable Futures • Refugee Resettlement • Poverty and Racism • Dysfunctional Schools*, and trying to figure out what to tell their grandfather what they thought of it.

So we're going to try and break it down.

Paulson, and his wife, Lisa, first ended up in the Plymouth area in 1970 when they bought 46 acres on County U from the William Miller family, then elderly, who had given up their dairy business to move to Plymouth. (This was the first tract sold once they subdivided their farm.) They had raised six kids in the turn-of-the-century farmhouse (with no indoor plumbing).

The Paulsons had a dream of creating an ecological school. During the next decades, they promoted a theme of "sustainability-oriented" topics. This included, in the mid-1990s, being part of a group attempting to design an ecovillage project at the Silver Springs trout farm (southwest of State 67 and County SS). The aim was to save that property from becoming a subdivision, but the plan was rejected by the town of Mitchell. This was when such ideas were still considered somewhat "radical thinking," before today's great concerns about climate change and depletion of natural resources, when even the term "sustainability" was largely unfamiliar in the mainstream.

In the 1960s Paulson organized the University of Wisconsin's first department to address inner city poverty and racism, and before that had been involved with societal turmoil in Europe and Latin America.

Paulson's *Odyssey* traces the evolution of many of these events, the book going back into his early life before he and Lisa arrived in Wisconsin, including their adventures in postwar Italy working with bombed-out Neapolitans, resettling Iron Curtain escapees on the island of Sardinia, and studying the relationship between politics and economic development in Brazil. While the book covers a long period, much of it focuses on larger questions that continue to drive current history and haunt us today. From time to time Lisa joins Belden to add her views on these issues.

ODYSSEY
How Should We Think about Haiti?

by Belden Paulson

B.J. Most of us haven't had the experience of being near anything like what we are now seeing and hearing about the earthquake that has devastated Haiti. It's hard to know how we should think about what to do. Here's what you wrote in your book, *Odyssey*, when, as a young man first confronting circumstances somewhat similar in the tragic post-World War II environment of the cave of Capodimonte, Italy, you were attempting to help distribute food to 39 families living there:

They are sick, physically and mentally and spiritually. The Capodimonte people are as low as one can go. They have nothing in life except their hordes of babies and rodents in their underground shacks. The municipal authorities have not bothered to repair water pipes. . . . There are tiny strings of lights so dim one would surely go blind reading for very long. When we began the distribution—and this food was supposed to be only for the children—a fight broke out. Soon a woman insulted and cursed a man who had lunged for the food, and the man kicked the woman, who was pregnant, in the stomach. She fell unconscious. People gathered around and mass chaos ensued. Quickly we picked up what was left of the food and escaped.

Q. What can a person faced with this kind of news, this kind of imagery of desperation and poverty do that matters? What kind of effort will be required by those trying to bring food and relief to Haiti?

A. When I arrived in Naples five years after the end of World War II, there were thousands of bombed-out Neapolitans living in caves and ruins. This was one of the worst slums in Western Europe. Hulks of destroyed vessels lined the harbor.

As a volunteer just out of college working with Teofilo Santi, a dedicated Italian doctor, an American colleague and I were assigned to bring food to the homeless cave dwellers. I had arranged with the U.S. Navy to give us surplus food from the ships to feed the starving.

After the traumatic incident in Capodimonte cave described above, I urged Dr. Santi to re-evaluate our work. Important as it was to keep the people alive, relief was no solution. We needed to use every ounce of our energy for longer-term solutions: finding other places for the cave dwellers to live and lining up even the simplest jobs. Above all, we needed a strategy to bring self-sufficiency.

Within a year, Dr. Santi and I and our small staff created a social settlement center right in the middle of where 20,000 of these home-less were concentrated. Called *Casa Mia* (My Home), we had a medical clinic, literacy and vocational classes. We fed 500 young people each day. But in my view, one our most sig-nificant efforts was the English class I taught where we brought to the center some of the more affluent folks in the city. On the surface it was a language class, but really it was con-sciousness-raising. Those people learned a lot. Also important was the soccer team we orga-nized that (with good coaching) won the city tournament. It brought these homeless youth into contact with other kids across the tracks and proved to them they could succeed. Of course, we also worked with the authorities to find housing and jobs for our families.

How does this relate to the Haiti earth-quake situation? At this moment the obvious overwhelming immediate need is relief: food, medicine, clean water, basic cleanup, finding any living souls still in the rubble, burying the dead.

Much relief is arriving to help. This is like the Capodimonte cave experience after the war but far worse.

The earthquake disaster offers a historic opportunity to attack Haiti's chronic poverty —one of the Western Hemisphere's worst.

As a sovereign nation, Haiti's government and people must be in charge, but here is an unprecedented opportunity for well-meaning resources from the outside—United Nations, U.S. government, NGOs (non-government organizations)—to not only help to rebuild the city (using renewable energy wherever possible), but to design and carry out a long-term strategy. This would include action to reorganize the educational system, draw in investment to establish small businesses (which was beginning to happen), mobilize some of the more affluent population from the unaffected region of the island, work with the authorities to create a new regime of civic leadership—and to overcome past corruption and dysfunctionality.

Too often catastrophic human situations momentarily attract abundant interest and resources, but these soon dry up. The status quo returns.

Is it only a dream that tomorrow's Haiti could become a showcase in the hemisphere because of enlightened leadership brought to bear on a sustained basis? Or will Haiti end up like Naples five years after the war, with homeless people still living in caves and an unresponsive surrounding society.

ODYSSEY
Do Aid Agencies Sometimes Prolong the Need for Assistance?

by Belden Paulson

B.J. While you were in post-World War II Italy, you decided to tackle the problem of Granili, the devastated waterfront slum of Naples, which the chief of the CARE mission to Italy said reminded him of Dante's "Purgatorio." You thought that a settlement house concept was a natural for this situation. By concentrating a medical clinic, educational programs for kindergarten to adults, craft schools, athletics, plus direct material assistance, a kind of part-time home for the people of Granili could be created. You found a building to rent and, with minimal conditions, became the first resident.

When you and your friends first opened the big iron gate, which promised a small measure of security, no one came. You later learned that:

> both a few communists and also Catholics had been at work. Apparently, the communist argument was that Americans had come to buy their souls with American dollars, while the Catholics' theme was that this was a Protestant initiative and people should be cautious with us—plus they should remember that the afterlife was far more significant than even these stressful conditions.

Q. This must have come as a surprise. What does this suggest about the reality that must be anticipated by aid workers and people of good will hoping to make a significant difference in places, for example, like Haiti? And, beyond that, how much of what we call humanitarian relief efforts might be called an ongoing benefit program for the providers themselves—to put it crudely, those who have their own livelihoods to defend, particularly those working at the upper levels of their organizations, like communists and the Catholic Church?

A. Most of the 20,000 miserable homeless people in Granili called themselves communist, but the communist leadership had little interest in solving the Granili problem. This would undermine their appeal, which depended on mass misery. As for the Catholics, Granili's birthrate was obscene, because about the only available free recreation was sex. The church focused on the afterlife, with little attention to the birthrate that accentuated the poverty.

I went to Granili and urged some families to check out our new center. It was not long before our facility was teeming with people of all ages. It was an oasis fostering a new life. Eventually the people found new places to live, Granili was torn down, and our center then relocated to another part of the city with other horrendous conditions.

A dozen years after World War II, I was back in Italy, this time to cofound a project to resettle "hard-core" refugees. The war had displaced 40 million people, but most of them had found new homes. However, some 40,000 were still stagnating in barbed-wire camps in several countries. With multiple handicaps, no one wanted them. Most authorities had given up, convinced that this residue of humanity was too far gone to ever become self-sufficient.

I knew a number of the refugees personally, as did my Naples colleague, Don Murray, who was now a film actor (he played opposite Marilyn Monroe in *Bus Stop*). Together, the two of us were determined to offer them a last chance. We bought virgin land on the island of Sardinia and created a small community for 15 families, based in farming and small industries. Some of the refugees became fully self-sufficient.

When I visited the camps to select the families, I soon found that these camps had become welfare institutions. The refugees had resigned themselves to permanent dependence. An infrastructure of vested interests had solidified with people whose jobs depended on *not* solving the problem. When I asked about a particular refugee family, the agency or the camp authority ashamedly pulled out a file that hadn't been dusted off for several years.

You might ask, what's this got to do with today's desperate Haiti situation? When there is great human tragedy, we don't ask questions. We go all out to help, we respect every agency working on the front line.

President Obama said: "We are mobilizing every element of our national capacity." Haiti has a proud past: it was the first independent nation in Latin America, it could boast a successful slave rebellion in 1804, and it has a rich culture.

But before the earthquake, Haiti was considered the poorest country in Latin America, its per capita GDP less than $800—two dollars per person per day. Although its more than a dozen universities produce a reservoir of college graduates, 80 percent emigrate (there are 600,000 Haitians in the U.S.). There's 50 percent illiteracy. The rich 1 percent reportedly own almost half of Haiti's wealth. Its Cité Soleil slum is considered one of the worst in the hemisphere. Half of the population of 10 million is under 20 years old; the country has one of the highest fertility rates in the Western Hemisphere. Some 98 percent of its once-lush forests have been cut and fertile lands destroyed, leading to desertification and flooding. Its modern political history is one of corruption and instability, foreign occupation and exploitation. In the current crisis, the government was invisible.

Foreign aid has been covering 30-40 percent of the government budget. Now, millions of dollars are flowing into the country, and the military of the U.S. and others have supplied thousands of troops to distribute aid and provide security. It's said that the NGO presence in Haiti per capita is higher than in any country in the world other than India. With huge long-standing chronic problems and a recent history of dependency on the outside, one can legitimately ask: what happened to all that financial and other assistance before the earthquake? Were there similar conditions to those we faced in Naples when in the beginning no one came to our center, or in the refugee camps where those personnel files gathered dust?

After Haiti's huge immediate relief operation subsides, the great recovery operation will begin. What a fantastic opportunity for the long-suffering people, for the government, and for all those NGOs, with plenty of international help already in the pipeline, to clear the decks and transcend the lethargy and vested interests of the past. They could build a new Haiti!

Will the weak government invite outside leadership to help design and implement a long-range plan? What about involving some of the rich who control the wealth? What about recruiting some of the thousands of professionals who emigrated, to return temporarily to help revitalize their original homeland? What about controlling the birthrate, a primary cause of the poverty? How about establishing standards for new construction that would more likely withstand the next earthquake or hurricane? What about reforesting and restoring the land, and working with the squatters and slum dwellers to become self-reliant in cooperating neighborhoods? What about imposing high ethical standards for all public employees? And working with outside investors who are indicating interest in Haiti? Some idealism, integrity, and commitment would do wonders.

Will it happen?

Bel and Lisa's 50th anniversary celebrated with family in Greece

February 2, 2010

ODYSSEY
Recipe for Living as a Couple

by Belden and Lisa Paulson

B.J. Now I would like to think that both of you are being interviewed. It's hard for me to imagine either of you without the other. As Lisa reported, when she and a friend tried to find Belden in the slum:

> We got lost but picked up quite a following of barefoot youngsters who seemed to recognize the one word we kept repeating, "Americano?" Suddenly the kids propelled us up to a high iron gate. They all shouted "BEL!"

That would have been the gate to a social assistance center dreamed up by Belden to help 500 people a day in a devastated waterfront slum in post-World War II Naples, Italy.

Later, Belden, you wrote home about Lisa to parents very worried about your situation in a tough place:

> . . . she's the kind of person who grows on you, at least on me . . . saw that I needed relaxation and very subtly helped me let down . . . noted that my habits were not the greatest . . . was wise enough not to speak unless she had something important to say . . . was a good critic of my writing . . . and her family seemed to have the same values as mine. She didn't push at all. You might almost think it had been planned!

Belden, your mother said, upon hearing that you would leave Naples to enter grad school and were planning marriage:

I have a big son who, with the rapidity with which he moves, takes the breath out of his family!

Lisa received the same response from her family. Or, as she wrote home:

If I had given any sign of being interested in him, he probably would have run. Then suddenly, after an enchanted evening and night of full moon, gondolas, and orchestras playing in Venice, we found ourselves discussing with the greatest ease what kind of wedding we wanted.

Then on one of your many waterfront walks along the Bay of Naples, you located a jewelry shop where you bought a simple ring,

which stands out as the cementing of a relationship that has lasted for more than fifty years.

Q. Since those romantic beginnings in Italy, the two of you have worked together on many projects. With Valentine's Day so near, what can you share about how you learned to function as a team, which may be of interest to young people contemplating life as a couple?

A. Belden. First, a little more about how we met and our early years, because this greatly influenced our later life. In future years when sometimes things got rough, those rich beginnings gave us tremendous staying strength.

Lisa. Armed with idealism and a backpack, I was roaming around Europe in 1952, looking for a way to help alleviate the terrible suffering and devastation following World War II. Running out of money in Rome, I looked up the office of the World Council of Churches; it was headed by a flamboyant White Russian, Prince Engalichev. He was intrigued by my

story, especially that I didn't care about making money—a kind of pre-Peace Corps orientation. When he mentioned one Belden Paulson working in the Naples ruins, a light bulb went on: I recognized Bel's name because we'd been classmates at Oberlin College, though never knew each other there. Immediately, I hopped on a train and headed south with no address, but encountered some of Bel's small barefoot clients who led me to his center, Casa Mia. The next day he agreed to take me on.

Belden. Our year together in the dire conditions of Naples proved we could uncomplainingly function in the worst possible environment. We were idealists, working as volunteers, with no compensation other than the satisfaction of alleviating needs. Lisa not only respected that for almost three years I had lived simply with no amenities; she happily joined in. Although *Casa Mia* was small, it was Italy's first social settlement center—with large, visible ramifications. It attracted people from all over. Lisa quickly grasped my proclivity for linking small creative projects to the challenges of large baffling problems.

We both also developed a great love for Italy that cemented a deep, lasting bond. We had continuing contact with people we knew in Italy. We could converse together in Italian. We rushed to Italian movies, and our first choice of cuisine usually was Mediterranean. Our first son, Eric, lived most of his early years in Italy; Steve, our second son, was born in Rome.

After eight years of marriage, the first really big bump in our relationship happened after I joined the University of Wisconsin in the early 1960s. I was fully engaged as a new faculty member, with classes and meetings in the community that took me away many nights and weekends. Lisa was home with two small children, suddenly a traditional suburban housewife. This was a far cry from our exciting cosmopolitan years living overseas, or even when she worked to support me while in grad school. Now, my work life barely involved her.

Lisa. These were my years of "malaise" when I imagined that I'd lost my sense of identity. Reading the new feminist, Betty Friedan, only exacerbated the frustrated feeling that I had no worthwhile profession, that I saw no outlet for my creative skills. I felt trapped and resentful.

Then, in 1971, it was finally my turn. There was an opportunity to help organize a school teaching altered states of consciousness, and soon I found myself speaking, writing, instructing, counseling. I was the one out every night while Bel had to rustle up meals for him and the kids. All of this happened over a long arc of time (with an important break in the latter 1960s when our family lived for a tumultuous year in Northeast Brazil). I point out that nowadays young people demand more immediate gratification.

Bel and I had recognized from the beginning that we were in it (whatever "it" was) for the long haul. First we had a decade of exciting joint adventures, mostly abroad. Then Bel spent much of the next 10 years climbing the academic ladder and gaining civic recognition while I mostly idled at home (though with a bit of a challenge to the grey cells when I helped him by translating and editing his first book, along with playing cello in the civic orchestra, and so on). Then in the first half of the 1970s, I was out in the limelight running classes, and he took on a chunk of the home responsibilities. It wasn't until the latter '70s, after I had visited Findhorn, the renowned spiritual/ecological

community in Scotland, and had brought back an idea for a huge local undertaking, that as a couple we came full circle—again working in tandem as full partners, fully committed to creating our own eco-community in rural Plymouth.

Belden. During my early university years, one of my main activities, typical for faculty, was writing for publication. I produced articles and monographs, and also a book, *The Searchers,* the story of Italy's most communist-voting village, where I lived for several months. I was constantly turning to Lisa as my critic and editor (not to mention typist of the final copy, before computers). Because I knew this was an imposition, I regularly offered to get outside help. Her response: no one else knows how your mind operates. Of course, I knew that no one could perform like her.

Over time we learned that in many facets of our lives—not only writing projects—we had amazingly complementary qualities. This organic relationship not only enhanced the effectiveness of various projects; it integrated our lives where the sum was truly greater than the individual parts. This complementarity flowered most of all when we cofounded the High Wind ecological community.

Lisa. Yes, probably the most important dynamic of our relationship has been discovering that we're so complementary in our skills and perceptions. Here's a good example, just this morning, of how this works. I'm just finishing writing my next book and had asked Bel to look over the final draft. Pencil in hand, he frowned over interpretations he didn't agree with, exactly as I do when I proofread his writing. We're both writers and come at our craft from very different viewpoints. We tend to pounce hard. We ridicule each other's work in a way that we might not tolerate from an outsider. And though feelings are wounded when we're attacked, we know the other is right and that we'd be in serious trouble if we didn't pay careful attention and make the necessary changes. We each want to be accurate and effective.

We value and cherish what the other brings to the table—to our life, our work, our practical partnership in all its facets. We know that we need both fact checker and poet; odd because I (the poet) am usually the detail person in everyday matters, while Bel is "big picture." Always these opposing qualities stand in healthy tension.

Our complementary approaches and perspectives have carried over into our social experiments where we've been a solid team, filling in the spaces the other doesn't see or isn't good at. In our High Wind community interactions, I was more a "process" person, while Bel tended to get impatient in long meetings, sometimes skimming obliviously over feelings of sensitive individuals in his eagerness to get to the important goals that others believed impossible. I might be passionate or reactive about an issue, where Bel remained calm, the peacemaker. Balancing our very different approaches proved valuable for a couple attempting to exercise leadership together.

Finally, in our personal life now, division of labor works well. Unlike most contemporary young couples, where household chores are shared equally, we found many years ago that we each possessed specific, unique talents and interests, quite opposite from the other. I wake up every morning, profoundly grateful for this person who effortlessly fills in my gaps and for whom I can return the favors with what comes more easily to me. Complementarity, as we've both said. And yes, we've found this definitely is a good recipe for love.

The Recipe . . .

Belden. To sum up what's been said above, our "recipe," in my view, comprises: our shared values on the deepest level, which includes many common interests, notwithstanding very different personalities; acceptance of the need for each of us to develop our own distinct identity, which nurtures our individual independence rather than dependence; while at the same time being fully aware of our fundamental interdependence, each of us knowing that our complementary abilities greatly enrich our relationship and our life together.

Ingredients for an enduring relationship . . .

Lisa. I affirm all that Bel says, concluding that our lives have indeed been filled with excitement, sparkle, great satisfactions and joy over a lot of years (we recently celebrated our 56th anniversary). In order to get to that place in a marriage or partnership, there are tips I'd offer:

Be kind: Allow the best traits/instincts of a mate to shine.

Indulge your partner: Encourage activities that he/she is passionate about, that bring delight, even if they aren't your thing.

Be patient: Recognize that there may be long arcs of experiences in a relationship, life events that balance out in the long run. One partner may have "innings" to shine for a while, and then they may switch. Admit to yourself that trouble may not always be the fault of the other; if you give up and walk away, the same problem is likely to surface with another partner.

Practice forbearance: Try not to be overly critical; bite your tongue. This is a challenge for a compulsive perfectionist like me whose proclivities and approaches are often opposite those of her mate. Be gentle! On the other hand, don't enable in toxic situations.

Be your own person: Don't let the attitude or behavior of a mate cripple your feelings of self worth. Don't be a doormat; you'll only end up a martyr. Both partners need to plan on together-time as well as time spent apart for perspective.

Bel and I are fortunate in that we've never been faced with what are sometimes major conflicts in relationships: we've never had to deal with abuse, alcohol or drug problems. We've never disagreed on how to allocate money, how to parent, or how to spend recreational time. We've always concurred absolutely on the values, purposes and goals in our life together. We're incredibly grateful now for all the precious experiences over so many years—the tough learning ones mixed in with the innumerable rich ones—watching our kids grow up, many family trips, great fun with friends around the world, individual and joint creative projects. In sum, finding the balance that affirms complementarity as well as wholeness in oneself is key.

Lisa. Barry (and Christie), Bel thinks all these warnings could scare young people away from even trying marriage! But they were certainly the lessons we learned (or at least recognized) over time that made possible the successful, happy relationship we've ended up with.

Palestinian refugee camp outside Bethlehem

ODYSSEY
Palestine Remains a Perennial Problem

by Belden Paulson

B.J. I trust that a story about two people who have a dream about what they can do is a dream well shared.

You are generously sharing yours in this very personal account of your lives. We have agreed to describe this process by my deriving questions from a memoir of your lives from your book, *Odyssey of a Practical Visionary: Eco-Communities • Sustainable Futures • Refugee Resettlement • Poverty and Racism • Dysfunctional Schools.*

At this point in our interviews about sustainability and creating a more livable world, Belden has survived a daring, post-college immersion in the slums of Italy where he has also met Lisa. (He hadn't really

thought much about the subject of women before.) He then realizes that he'd better get serious about his formal education, and about Lisa. So, partly due to connections but mostly because of his boots-on-the-ground experiments, he gets admitted at the last minute to the prestigious University of Chicago in political science. Before leaving Italy, he and Lisa together buy

a 70-piece set of rustic dishes with hand-painted peasant designs....

He also buys a unique ring in a back-street Naples jewelry shop that "stands out as the cementing of a relationship that now has lasted for more than fifty years."

Then, while working toward a doctorate and having his first son (Eric), Belden meets a university student from Jordan who says:

The official Arab position is that the Arab governments want NO settlement of the Palestinian problem now or in the foreseeable future. By biding their time and increasing their militancy, eventually they will bankrupt Israel and sap its strength.

The student tells him the root of the problem is not the refugees, although publicly it is, but national pride, demanding defeat of the Jews. Bel says in his book,

As I write this now, it seems incredible that this conversation took place more than 50 years ago, and that the exact same problem remains.

Q. (Actually, two questions.) What was the household division of labor like when you were going for an advanced degree?

And, if you could find yourselves back again in that conversation about the Palestinians and Israel, what would you say about the Arab wait-em-out strategy? Most importantly, what strategy would you suggest all parties now try?

A. We arrived at the university almost penniless, having served in Italy as volunteers. We rented a two-room prefab "hut" in the "rabbit patch" where fellow married students were lodged (so-called because many children resulted), for which we paid $48 a month, including utilities and heat.

Lisa was hired at the university personnel office, finding jobs for students. Later she found a great one for me, assisting the CBS radio staff to cover the 1956 Democratic national convention in Chicago (with Walter Cronkite, Eric Severaid, et al).

While Lisa was the main breadwinner, and by mutual agreement ran the household, apart from my rigorous studies I soon landed a research position with two other grad students to write a history of Kashmir. I knew nothing on the subject, but we combed every book in the university library. We petitioned our professor boss to send us to Kashmir but, unhappily, he had no funds.

Along the way, we faced three big interruptions. The first was academic. In those days, to finish all the Ph.D. work before writing your dissertation, you took four comprehensive four-hour exams, within several days. I passed the first three with flying colors, but the fourth was a bummer. The grading prof, an émigré from Germany whose English comprehension was not the best, apparently could not read my handwriting (admittedly nearly illegible), and he didn't pass me. To qualify for going on with the Ph.D., I had to take all four exams over again. I changed my subject and later did snag the degree.

Our second interruption ushered in an exciting new venture; at the time we had no clue that it would be life changing. My successor from Naples days, Don Murray, now a successful actor, stopped by our prefab and the three of us sat up most of the night reminiscing about Italy. Don was in Chicago to publicize his new film, *Bus Stop*, starring opposite Marilyn Monroe.

With some money in his pocket, instead of moving to Hollywood he wanted to return to Italy to help solve the "hard-core" refugee problem, and he wanted me to join him. (Part of our work in Naples had included doing relief work in the refugee camps.) We knew there were thousands of displaced persons (DP's) left over from the war plus escapees from communism in eastern Europe still stagnating in these barbed wire camps—now more than ten years after the war. Although most world authorities had given up hope of any solution, we believed that with a creative project, at least some of them could become self-sufficient. But meantime I had a Ph.D. to finish.

We'd just experienced a third interruption, wonderful as it was. Two weeks before, Lisa had given birth to Eric. Our first priority now had to be to take care of our new family. During the next year this combination of family matters, the Ph.D., and Don's proposed project presented formidable challenges.

One of our recreations at the university was to visit International House, where many of the foreign students lived. My sister Polly, a theology student, was president there and knew all the residents. Because Lisa and I had visited a refugee camp in Jordan on our trip to the Middle East before leaving Naples, she urged us to meet several Arab grad students. I found them very reluctant to talk; they feared that if they expressed their views publicly, they'd lose their scholarships. They assumed all Americans were pro-Jewish, and they knew that some of the university's most distinguished professors were Jews who had escaped from Nazi Germany. Finally, I showed them a large, beautiful hand-drawn poster with Arabic poetry given us in the refugee camp in Jericho. It showed a map of the land now in Israel that this particular refugee had once owned. At that point the students really opened up.

We said we had spent several hours in the camp and were very sympathetic to the cruel Arab refugee situation. Thousands continued to exist in the camps in appalling conditions (today, there are more than a million). These were people who had once lived in Palestine and then, for a multitude of complex reasons, had left when the new state of Israel was established by the United Nations in 1947-48. Lisa

and I made clear that we personally were neither pro-Jewish nor pro-Arab; we simply wanted to see peace achieved. These students said the only way to resolve the problem would be for all the refugees to return to their former lands, now part of Israel. This will never happen; thus, the perpetuation of the camps.

When Don Murray and I organized our project in Sardinia to resettle refugees stagnating in camps in Italy (these were Eastern European, not Arab refugees), we created a strategy that eventually won the support of both the U.N. and the Italian government. We suggested that we buy and develop land and small industries in one of the country's most depressed areas (the island of Sardinia), helping both the participating refugees *and* the surrounding region. The plan was accepted and we created jobs for the refugees and the local Italians. The project's net impact brought benefits to both populations.

The Italian authorities, facing their own huge unemployment problem, and also very worried about domestic communism, had little interest in bringing refugees from other countries into their economy. Further, these anti-communist refugees were considered an internal threat to the large communist constituency in Italy. However, the government saw value in our approach of providing local jobs and new technology even though we were using the refugees to enhance the depressed region. The U.N. high commissioner for refugees, on the other hand, had no particular interest in contributing to the Italian economy unless this contributed directly to refugee resettlement, as happened with our project. An added important factor was that Sardinia was almost unique in that it was probably the only *under-populated* part of Italy—its numbers decimated by malaria (then wiped out after the war by the Rockefeller Foundation).

The government was encouraging new settlement there.

While working in Sardinia, and later with the U.N., I found surprising interest among top officials in utilizing our model with the Arab refugees. Although our project was small in size, it had obvious visible relevance for the massive problem of the refugees now stagnating in the camps of Jordan, Syria and Lebanon. I wrote a "Proposal for Pilot Project to Resettle Arab Refugees Now in Camps in an Underdeveloped Area of the Near East." Senator Hubert Humphrey wrote to me, as did an official of the U.S. State Department, a senior official of UNHCR in Geneva, and the head of the Near East Christian Council for Refugee Work in Jerusalem. I surmised that they liked our ideas that were based on practical experience. Given all my other responsibilities at the time, however, I wasn't able to follow through with this expressed interest.

I sense that the situation has not fundamentally changed from the time of that conversation at the University of Chicago in the mid-1950s. Eventually, a Mandela-type leader may emerge who will rise above the historic emotions set in concrete by all sides to find a solution to this great unresolved political conflict and human tragedy. (In the past, valiant peace efforts were made by Anwar al-Sadat of Egypt and Rabin of Israel, but they were both assassinated.) At a minimum, I expect peace will include these ingredients: 1) recognition of Israel's right to exist within the borders agreed to by the U.N. Security Council Resolution 242 (that is, giving up lands acquired from the war of 1967, with some accommodation of Israeli settlements in the West Bank); 2) establishment of a Palestinian state with recognized national borders; 3) some sort of international jurisdiction for Jerusalem, a place of sacred historic importance for both Jews and Arabs; 4) resettlement of most Arab refugees now in the camps in Arab lands, probably with a strategy similar to that used in our Sardinia project (a few refugees may return to Israel but most will go elsewhere); 5) massive international financial assistance and political support and guarantees to support implementation.

Background for
ODYSSEY

By Barry Johanson

The "Odyssey" series currently appearing in *The Review* is a unique, long-term interview with Belden and Lisa Paulson. The interview is based on Belden's memoir, *Odyssey of a Practical Visionary.*

It's a love story. It's about a couple unusually inquisitive about what ails us. It's not about how to think or what to do. It's about wondering, then trying. They have the credentials to back up what they say.

The format for the series is itself innovative. *Review* Publisher Barry Johanson met the Paulsons many years ago when the woods, hills, fields, streams, and ponds of Sheboygan County's town of Mitchell stole their hearts away.

In the "Odyssey" series, Barry extracts and emails questions related to the memoir. Belden and/or Lisa respond. Each of the couple is a gifted writer, so the answers being published have a quality often absent in the shoot-from-the-lip, partisan hissing of today's political, blogging or digital comment.

The Paulsons, who have just celebrated their 56th wedding anniversary because they agreed to "stick with it, whatever 'it' was," have painstakingly constructed closely examined lives trying to identify who is in the lineup of global thugs with names like poverty, war, intolerance, and environmental dismemberment.

Many of us have shared dreams of doing something concrete and personal to rid our streets of such abominations. Uniquely, the Paulsons kept an extraordinary file of their daily pursuits—successes and failures—which they then devoted a decade to sort through, organize, write, critique and publish. What became several books was first conceived as a letter to four grandchildren.

Compare that effort with what we are told about so many of today's headline makers who are used because they have svelte bodies, or have excelled at their craft, or at athletics, acting, or political posturing, or any of the other fun excitations we have every right to enjoy.

The Paulsons' situation is not too unusual to be true, and is somewhat more like the problem of the famous poet W.H. Auden when he was asked to return to Oxford and take up residence in a cottage at Christ College.

As the Scottish novelist Alexander McCall Smith put it:

> *It had been hoped that Auden would sit in a coffee shop and undergraduates would come up and engage him in (for them) intelligent conversation. Auden was willing to sit in the coffee shop, and did so, but very few people plucked up the courage to go sit at his table and talk to him. So mostly he sat alone. How sad, and what opportunities were lost!*

Our "Odyssey" column is somewhat comparable to Auden's table setting in a coffee shop.

We have an opportunity to ask questions for which it's highly more likely than not that there will be carefully articulated answers, or at least intriguing observations.

At the conclusion of Homer's classic story, "Odyssey," an oar is planted in the sand, so that it may sprout and become a tree. That image would be a fitting symbol for this *Odyssey of a Practical Visionary* (available at www. Thistlebooks.com). Any questions related to it will be forwarded to the Paulsons and should be directed to reply@plymouth-review.com.

Eavesdrop only, or join the conversation.

Steve, flanked by his kids in southern France

FEBRUARY 16, 2010

ODYSSEY
First Responder Breathes Life into a Parent's Memoir

by Belden Paulson

B.J. In these interviews so far we have just begun to broach the subjects of love, marriage, and then children—Eric coming first, and later, Steve.

Christie and I have a sense of what Steve is like through listening to his wonderful Wisconsin Public Radio interview program "To the Best of Our Knowledge."

During one recent segment, Steve interviewed a musician filming a documentary about his father, a visionary physicist, which he said was the luckiest thing any son could do.

Belden, you credit Steve with being critically helpful in editing and creating your *Odyssey of a Practical Visionary*, a print documentary about both his parents.

Q. How would you describe his role in the process of writing the book?

A. Our son Steve is a PBS radio producer, winning national Peabody and Templeton awards. As a tough-minded journalist, he was an ideal "first-responder," someone who would take a hard look at my book when it was still open-ended raw material.

As a personal memoir, my original intention was to write down whatever information about my life that I thought worth preserving—taken from accumulated letters and documents—before throwing away what was left. Since over the years I had helped to clean out six attics of family and relatives, some materials going back more than a century, I had filled many dumpsters. I knew that once Lisa and I checked out, our kids would probably be merciless: they'd "sensibly" toss out all of our "valuable" records.

As I continued to write, I gave Steve over a thousand pages, which he dutifully read, over a period of several months.

His first question: who is going to read all of this? Who is your audience? He said: important as it is to you, no one really cares about all the classes you taught, talks you gave, articles you wrote, memos you prepared. People are interested in stories, conflicts, motivations, crucial relationships, failures as well as successes, significant turning points in your life journey.

A few days ago, at your request, I asked Steve to send a couple of paragraphs recalling his early reactions in the editing process. He replied:

One of the remarkable features of my father's book is the wealth of primary documents he was able to cite—printed articles, position papers and, above all, letters. The earliest drafts of the book tended to quote these documents at great length. As one of the first readers, I saw that my primary role was to push for various cuts in order to streamline the narrative.

For me, the great pleasure of reading the book was discovering how various pieces of my parents' lives fit together. Of course, I'd already heard most of the stories. But until I read the book, I never really understood how my dad's earliest experiences in Italy—his church-sponsored work in the slums of Naples—related to his later life, particularly his work with High Wind. I came to see a strong spiritual current that has run throughout

his life. It was striking to me how he, as the grandson of a missionary, came to play the role of 'missionary' himself in some of his later ecological and spiritual endeavors. Because he didn't spell out these connections in the early drafts of the book, I urged him to make them more explicit in his conclusion.

As an aside, I'll add that this led to some long and invigorating conversations—especially as I worked on my own book about science and religion—about the similarities and differences between 'spirituality' and 'religion.' [NOTE: Oxford University Press is publishing his book later this year, which encompasses interviews with leading world thinkers.] *I suppose that's been the best thing about my dad's book. Reading it turned out to be a family affair, and it has made all of us reflect on how our lives have taken the particular shapes they have.*

This, indeed, has been a family enterprise. The seed was planted when my sister, Polly, gave me a little known publication about our ancestor, William Henry, born in 1728. He ended up a gunsmith in George Washington's army. He served in the Continental Congress. The book details how he hosted at his home such famous American Revolutionary War figures as Thomas Paine.

As I pondered my own life adventures, I thought that the day might arrive when my four grandchildren would ask: "What was my grandfather like? How was it that he just happened to be present and participated in various ways in some of the great events of the last half of the 20th century?" They might find a few hours in a quiet place to read, raising such questions, but by then Lisa and I might have checked out.

First, I simply decided to write a long letter to the grandchildren—not considering publication. When friends and colleagues heard about this "long letter," they wanted a copy. Eventually it turned into a book.

The first person to read every line of the some 750-page tome was our grandson, Niko, Eric's son. Based in Washington, D.C., Niko visited us shortly after publication last July. He had the book in hand every spare minute. On driving trips the weighty volume (three and a half pounds) rested on his lap.

Each chapter stimulated dialogue; he wanted details that could pertain to where his own life was heading. As a brilliant young intellectual, and skeptical (like me), he probed for far more than what I had written. His questions and comments, coming from his generation's world, would have enriched the book.

What a blessing I was around for this conversation, instead of Niko unearthing a dusty memoir years later—when perhaps he'd be clearing out our attic!

ODYSSEY
Waging War for Hearts and Minds

by Belden Paulson

B.J. Most young people today, say those under 30, have little conception of the fears generated by the Cold War. This was the four-decade period roughly from the end of the 1940s to the end of the 1980s. You were working among the post-World War II homeless in Europe during much of the 1950s. You were being told that Stalin's communist armies, still fully mobilized after the end of the war while our forces were demobilizing, could easily march across Western Europe, not unlike Hitler's Nazi army a short time before.

For personal reasons, you did a lot of thinking in those days about the military.

Q. Could you describe the detailed plan you wrote titled "Soldiers of Understanding"? What brought this about? How has the concept fared? Having experienced what has happened in the past 50 years since it was written, what, if anything, would you change or add?

A. Working in Italy, I saw how the Italian Communist Party, leader of the Left coalition, nearly won several elections. It would have been the first western country where communists took over through free elections. Most of the people I worked with in the postwar slums of Naples were communist, although they had little idea what

this meant. A few of their leaders had visited the Soviet Union. I got to know many officers and sailors of the American Sixth Fleet headquartered in Naples, and they took very seriously their responsibility for guarding western democracy on Europe's southern flank.

Soon after graduating from high school in 1945, I was drafted into the Navy. Since World War II had just ended and America was demobilizing, and I had no interest in a military career, I only served for nine months. Then in 1950 the Korean War broke out and the draft was reinstated. It turned out that I was still draft-eligible because I had served less than one year. The overseas arm of the Congregational Church, which was supporting our work, eventually convinced the draft board that my voluntary service in Naples was more valuable to the national interest than my rejoining the military and I was granted a deferment.

Our work became a magnet for international attention. Although I always described my activities as compassionate efforts to help homeless war victims in dire need, many observers argued that I was a visible example of someone "on the front line fighting communism." I was meeting regularly with people from the American Embassy and "visiting firemen" from all over. They publicized our activities as "confronting grassroots communism." Even experts who had worked in Asia saw our work as a viable model for blunting the communist mass appeal there. My later efforts in Italy, which included living in the most communist voting village of Italy, only enhanced this image of my work.

Even during the period when it was likely I'd be drafted again, I began reflecting on the role of the military. While I understood the critical responsibility of the American Fleet, I also knew that the military could not implement the humanitarian work I was doing. (We had created Casa Mia, a social assistance center in the midst of the worst ruins, with multiple services for hundreds every day.) The United States and its allies badly needed to direct a response to the heart of the communist appeal—a response that would help eradicate the misery, demonstrate our understanding of the problems, and actively participate in effective problem solving.

People pushed me to write up my ideas, which resulted in a paper titled "Soldiers of Understanding." The basic idea was that the Selective Service would be given authority to pick young men (later also women) of draft age for the kind of humanitarian service in which I was engaged because it served the national interest. While I respected conscientious objectors who refused the military for religious reasons, this new role would be a government mandate, an alternative to the military, dedicated to human needs. Participants would be trained to serve in areas of high tension, either directly under government auspices or assigned to other appropriate organizations. They would also gain terrific overseas experience—valuable assets for America's future. Various leaders urged me to submit my plan to the secretary of state and other authorities. Once my deferment in

Naples was granted, however, I got so bogged down with work that I didn't follow through with this proposal.

Almost a decade later, after more years of grassroots experience, including almost two years with the United Nations in Rome, I utilized the "Soldiers" paper along with other subsequent experience, to write a "Proposal for a Foreign Aid Program that could have Effective Results." This no longer involved Selective Service or the military, but dealt with working at the grassroots. It called for a chain of pilot projects in the emerging low-income countries to train local leaders. It emphasized the need to understand the dynamics of village problems, especially the deeper structural issues, identifying breakthrough points, working with and building trust among indigenous elements, and linking local resources with larger outside resources. This was still at the height of the Cold War, when communism was finding fertile environments in Asia, Latin America and Africa. Conversely, our government's policies were often considered unresponsive or insensitive, based largely on money and military power. I still felt there was a place for Selective Service and the military, to provide a cadre of personnel trained for humanitarian-type service, but it had become obvious that complete separation from the military, and even from the government, had distinct advantages.

Lisa sent my proposal to Gordon Boyce, head of the Experiment in International Living, with whom she had worked for two years before meeting me. As a close friend of Sargent Shriver, who was soon to become President John Kennedy's first director of the Peace Corps, Boyce replied to Lisa. He liked my proposal and said it had arrived at "an extremely opportune time." He was just leaving for Washington for a Peace Corps planning meeting. He said the plan showed

> *remarkable cogency and purposefulness. Bel's remarks have already reached the President's desk . . . I had the opportunity to interject some of Bel's philosophy and suggestions where, I have every reason to believe, they will do the most good.*

The Peace Corps is government-sponsored and financed, but is completely separate from the military and tries to maintain its independence from government foreign policy generally.

When I finally left Italy, Senator Hubert Humphrey, prominent on the Foreign Relations Committee, who had followed my work and the ideas in my proposals, was urging me to join a new American aid program being launched in Latin America. Called the "Alliance for Progress," it would employ me as a community development adviser in Northeast Brazil, a region of mounting ferment and great economic need. In the ensuing discussions, my foreign aid ideas were fully aired,

but eventually (and luckily), I ended up not with the government, but at the University of Wisconsin-Milwaukee.

One of my early university assignments was to help prepare a proposal for the university to become one of the first training centers in the country for Peace Corps volunteers. My "Foreign Aid" proposal was used and, happily, UWM was selected as a new training facility. I served as the first training project director, for volunteers destined to work in Peru.

As a final comment about this circuitous story that evolved from the "Soldiers of Understanding" proposal in the early 1950s, I am convinced that one of the most worthwhile strategies we can pursue today in Afghanistan relates to the ideas we've been discussing. With well-trained people, working both in the military and on the outside, addressing real needs in the villages, there is hope for an eventual positive outcome that would be beneficial to the local people and the U.S.

Don Murray and Bel at the refugee project in Sardinia

MARCH 2, 2010

ODYSSEY
Partnering with a Movie Star to Save Refugees

by Belden Paulson

B.J. You had a close friend, Don Murray, an actor who played in *Bus Stop* with Marilyn Monroe, and then went on to starring roles in other major films.

Q. What was Don Murray like? And, what is it like when what we now call a "celebrity" is part of real life—your life?

A. When I learned in latter 1956 that Don Murray had just finished the movie *Bus Stop* with Marilyn Monroe, I was very proud of him, not only for the film but because he publicly announced that he intended to use his new stardom to help resolve the refugee problem in Europe. I wrote to congratulate

him on his success and especially on his commitment to refugees.

Soon thereafter, when he came to Chicago on a publicity trip, he called me. Lisa and I were hunkered down in our prefab at the University of Chicago where I was sweating out my Ph.D. studies. We sat up most of a night reminiscing about our work in Italy. Before leaving, he urged me to return to Italy with him to help move refugees out of the camps. Since I had developed some ideas about this, I said I'd assist with a study, but my first priorities now were taking care of our two-week-old Eric and the Ph.D.

I had first met Don when he followed me as a volunteer working with homeless Italians in Naples. Both of us were in our early twenties, and he was to replace me as director of our social settlement center, Casa Mia. He was serving his two years of alternative service as a C.O. (conscientious objector) with the peace group, Church of the Brethren. For several days before Lisa and I left Naples, I introduced him to the surrounding wartime ruins and our intensive operation. We also visited the barbed-wire camps where escapees from communist Eastern Europe were still stranded, perhaps for life.

My next contact with Don, about a year later, was on a trip to New York when I learned from the Congregational Christian Service Committee, which supported our Naples work, that Don was having big difficulties. He had contracted yellow jaundice, and through unexpected political maneuvering, he never became Casa Mia director. He wrote me: "This is the most difficult, exasperating and discouraging eight months that I ever hope to see." He ended up spending much of his time in the refugee camps, appalled by the "hopeless imprisonment of guiltless people." He began to write a movie script about a service worker and a refugee girl.

I knew Don had done bit-part acting on Broadway but had no idea about his movie career. Some days after his Chicago visit, he called from New York, urging me to come east to meet him and Hope Lange (his actress wife, also in *Bus Stop*). They were about to leave for Europe on film business, but while there they expected to explore the potential support for a refugee project. I flew out and the three of us began to hatch a plan.

On New Year's Eve, 1956, he called from Hollywood to report on his and Hope's Europe trip. The United Nations authorities in Geneva and the Italian government in Rome had both given the green light for a project.

At our next session in New York at the end of January—every free minute when he was not shooting a movie—we got down to details. Were a project to result, Don and Hope would be co-chairs, I'd be project director, and the two church organizations close to us would provide administrative backup. Both Lisa's parents and mine hoped and prayed that no project would materialize; they thought it essential that I finish the Ph.D. and get a regular job.

In April Don called to say that his latest film, *Bachelor Party*, would be featured at the Cannes Film Festival in France in early May. He exchanged his first-class air ticket for two tourist seats, and we both flew to Italy. After making some initial surveys together and talking to several refugees we personally knew in the camps, he had to return to Hollywood. Luck was with us, however, and there were startling results: 1) We found that if we bought land on the island of Sardinia and agreed to create an innovative project there to resettle 15 families from the camps, the Italian Ministry of Interior would give all the necessary permissions, and the development agencies interested in this depressed area would provide generous subsidies; and 2) If we could figure out how to rehabilitate these "hard core" refugees who had been stagnating for 10 years or more in camps, who'd been given up on by most world authorities, we'd receive heavy financial backing from the U.N. High Commissioner for Refugees.

These, of course, were two big "ifs" since to date no one had pulled off such a plan. The agencies appreciated our idealism but argued that our project was a HUGE gamble for everyone, as well as for the two of us personally. Don and Hope were in the early stages of promising acting careers. This complex undertaking would prove an enormous career distraction, not to mention a serious personal financial risk. Don had agreed to put up the start-up capital: initially $50,000 to buy the land and at least another $50,000 to begin operations until we could pull in the subsidies. At that point he had very little idea where to find the money.

The rest is history: the project worked, more or less as planned. When we faced financial desperation, Don arranged with NBC television to get us on the *This Is Your Life* show where we raised $90,000; people cared enough to send us 40,000 letters. (It was about my life, but Don, Hope, Lisa, the U.N. Deputy High Commissioner for Refugees from Geneva and others all appeared on the program.) Subsequently, I was hired by the UNHCR for almost two more years to help clear the camps in Italy. The policy implications resulting from our experiment were widespread in refugee circles.

I never thought of Don as a celebrity. As when we first met in Naples, we just saw ourselves as two young idealists with dreams and a lot of determination. We believed we could make the world better by attacking one of its great humanitarian problems. Although we lacked the credentials of more experienced professionals, we had a couple of advantages: we personally knew a number of the refugees and had built at least some minimal mutual trust, and we didn't accept the word "impossible." Certainly, we never would have had a chance without Don's star status; I was always impressed at how we were able to move through impenetrable bureaucracies. Also, we had a naiveté that actually served to our advantage; at one point I asked the mental health adviser with the U.N. High Commissioner for

Refugees how we were able to deal successfully with these difficult refugees when most others had failed. His response: You started with the assumption that they could make it. You didn't know how many different plans had been tried and had failed.

When we met with reporters, whether in New York or Italy, their first question to Don usually was: What's it like to kiss Marilyn Monroe? They soon found that these "glamour" questions held no interest for him; he'd talk about his philosophy of life and refugees. In the early period after he had made several films and was considered one of the brightest new stars in Hollywood, he was constantly pushing the press and the gossip columns to write about our project, about which they had zero interest. When they did, their comments had grandiose exaggerations and inaccuracies. For example, when pundit Hedda Hopper wrote about how our project had already become "worldwide" in scope before we even owned land and had not as yet received any official permissions, I voiced strong displeasure. Don replied that we needed to decide whether we wanted to tap into the publicity that the entertainment "Magic Lantern" world offered:

> *Hedda Hopper's estimated 25,000,000 readers don't give a hoot about refugees . . . They don't care what the problem is or what is being done to solve the problem . . . If you choose to benefit from ties to filmland, just prepare to accept the slings and arrows of outrageous articles. . . .*

We decided we had no choice but to go along. Even inaccurate publicity was better than none.

Bel with Don and volunteer staff on the land in Sardinia

MARCH 4, 2010

ODYSSEY
Frontline Work with an Actor

by Belden Paulson and Lisa Paulson

Q. *What was* Don Murray *like? And, what is it like when what we now call a "celebrity" is part of real life?*

A. Belden. Along the way, deep into the refugee resettlement project in Sardinia, both Don's family and mine faced rough stretches, and I suppose we wondered whether all the challenges were worth it. Lisa contracted a serious case of hepatitis and almost died, forcing us to be separated for seven months while she recuperated back in the U.S. For a prolonged period after the project had been going for a couple of years, Don had no film contracts and was severely stretched financially. When I stayed at his and Hope's home during the *This Is Your Life* episode in 1958, I saw that their house had little furniture; most of their money was poured into the project. Eventually Don and Hope split, probably in part because of the heavy burden their commitment entailed.

In the project's first half year, we recognized that what the authorities had been telling us might be accurate, that maybe after the long years in camp, the refugees were incapable of becoming self-sufficient. Failure loomed as a real possibility.

In one of his letters Don wrote me:

Basically, what we are doing in this project is not only trying to establish a pattern for settling refugees generally, but we are bearing witness to our Christian faith in the ability of the human spirit to change.

So far we have not seen this change too evident in the refugees, but I know that so long as we keep our faith strong, this change must one day come. If it doesn't happen with these refugees, it will happen for some others. If you [referring to our Sardinia crew] could only see what strength you give me. . . . I think you would have an even greater conviction of the worth of your work, even though you do not see the results you first expected. . . .

I believe for the first time that even out here (in Hollywood) we are finally beginning to make a dent on the conscience of a conscience-hardened world.

Happily, conditions did change and we felt we did achieve the essential objective that had motivated us from the start—to provide a model for the rehabilitation and economic integration of hard-core refugees. As Don wrote after reading my book about our project:

In resettling refugees from World War II, Belden and I shared an enterprise unmatched in creativity, challenge, travail, disaster, and triumph by any stage or film drama of my career. I still wonder how we had the audacity to aspire to salvage lives that "experts'"had abandoned. In a depressed and tumultuous environment, we achieved what was deemed unachievable.

Lisa remembers several episodes in our collaboration with Don:

Lisa.

- For a few moments I experienced what it's like for a celebrity to be hounded by an insatiable public or rapacious paparazzi. Don and I had arrived in Simaxis, the small Sardinian village where our

refugee settlement was located. We were trying to cross the main street to get to the rickety movie house where Don's film, *Bus Stop,*was to be shown. The villagers spotted Don approaching and lunged *en masse* at us in a frenzy of excitement—"Here comes OUR hero!" The crush was so intense that we couldn't move; I panicked, fearing briefly we might be trampled by the screaming mob. But we fought our way through, as Don, beaming, reached out to take the hands thrust at him, and then he gave a lovely heartfelt talk (in Italian) in the theater.

- On that trip, as always, Don stayed at our simple apartment on a dusty back alley. Here he was anything but the film star as we wrestled with the latest conflict among the refugees or worried over how we could come up with funds to keep the project afloat. Toward the end of his week's stay, Don and I discovered, somewhat to our horror, and then amusement, that inadvertently we'd been sharing the same toothbrush in our one bathroom (we had identical brushes). You can't get much more intimately connected to celebrity than that!

- Just after *This Is Your Life*, I came down with hepatitis. I was still in the U.S., but Bel had been anxious to get back to Sardinia to the refugees and our 18-month-old son, Eric, and had flown on ahead. I was told I wouldn't be healed enough to leave the country for at least six months, so four months later Don became so concerned about Eric being stranded in Europe without his mother—knowing also that his care placed a huge responsibility on Bel, who was already stressed to the limit wrestling with the constant crises with the project—that he flew over to get him. When he delivered Eric to my parents in the New York airport, Don reported that Eric had snuggled like an angel on his chest the whole way, happily submitting to having his diapers changed and going to sleep contentedly with his bottle. Again, here was the extraordinarily empathetic, loving, unpretentious human being, not one who ever let his professional success go to his head.

- A year later we were in New York to plan with Don and his wife Hope, and also to report in to the CCSC [the Congregational Service Committee] that was contributing Bel's small ($4,000 a year) stipend. After our very informal relationship with these two close friends, it was always startling to see the effect Don had on the heads of the church groups (and also on the U.N. officials he met with in Geneva, Switzerland). They turned into shy, star-struck fans and—luckily for us—were often mesmerized into proffering aid of various sorts. While in New York, we once found ourselves chatting with actor Montgomery Clift in the elevator going up to Don and Hope's hotel apartment, such was our strange existence that spanned two very different worlds. I recall, also, how Don,

desperate to break free from sequestering Bel in Beverly Hills so he could rehearse in Hollywood with the rest of us in the week before *This Is Your Life*, arranged for Bel to spend a couple of days being entertained by his pals Eva Marie Saint and Shirley MacLaine.

- A final vignette: Years later, in the early 1970s, we visited Don and his new wife Bette at their Long Island home. Being heavily involved in a Milwaukee school teaching altered states of consciousness, I volunteered to put Don into hypnosis. His whole family crowded around excitedly as I quietly talked him down. As an actor who was accustomed to living much of his professional life in his imagination, Don was the ideal subject. He responded immediately to suggestions that he was traveling to a bucolic scene in nature, a place of healing and peace. I realized that it was this gift of being able to visualize a better world that made him the perfect partner for Bel, who shared this same proclivity for creatively imagining the future, so that together they were able to bring off the refugee project in Sardinia. And like Bel, Don continues to exercise his creative muscle; he writes scripts about topics he believes in and is still acting in films.

ODYSSEY
A Pilot Solution for Refugees Trapped in Camps

by Belden Paulson

B.J. You use the terms *refugee psychology* and *hard-core refugees.*

   And you say,

   Today, decades later, there are even more millions of refugees in the world stagnating in camps, and resolution of the problem will require similar kinds of hard data and imaginative policy alternatives.

Q. What do you mean?

A. These questions deal with fairly complex situations. Unhappily, many folks I worked with in the refugee field never did grasp the idea of refugee psychology, which definitely reduced their effectiveness.

Mario's story presents both the problem and the solution.

Mario was a Yugoslav in his 30s. He had been chased by both the Nazis and Tito's communists as he fled into Italy at the end of World War II. Having been rejected by numerous emigration commissions for health reasons (he had lost a lung to tuberculosis), Mario was one of the many refugees who were probably doomed to spend the rest of their days in a camp. It was 1957 when Don Murray and I first met him; he had already been there for 12 years. The camp was enclosed by barbed wire, to keep the refugees in and local, desperately poor Italians out.

Mario was part of the so-called *hard-core* (refugees considered non-resettleable). He had been screened again and again. Now when an emigration official from the U.S. or another country sat down to interview him, he'd say: "Don't bother, you're wasting your time because the answer will be 'No.'" He'd been checked by social workers and psychologists, and no matter what solution had been proposed, he was still in camp. Over 40 million Europeans had been displaced by the war, and millions more were fleeing their home countries coming under communist domination. A U.N. document described the situation as the largest population displacement in human history, concluding: "the refugee constitutes the largest humanitarian issue of our time."

By the time Don Murray and I decided to create a project in Italy, there were still 40,000 hard-core refugees left in camps throughout Europe, including several thousand in five camps around Naples. All the rest had emigrated to find new homes, or had arranged to return to their former countries, or had found ways to integrate into the country where the camp was located. In the case of Italy, this was almost impossible because of chronic unemployment. Further, Italy was threatened by a strong, domestic communist party and the government was reluctant to resettle escapees who were virulently anti-communist.

We found that Mario had learned to adapt to life in camp, as had Roubal and Nyc, two long-time refugees from Czechoslovakia, and the many others we came to know from such countries as Hungary, Bulgaria, Albania, and even Spain. They had learned to play the system, to exploit whatever resources were accessible in the camp, and this could include other inmates. Although we didn't know their individual roles, we did know there were various small businesses in the camps based in gambling, prostitution rings, and the like. All the refugees had begun to conclude that they would live out their lives in camps.

As plans for resettlement on the island of Sardinia began, I wrote to Don in Hollywood:

> We're dealing with people who have been broken, cast almost completely out of the orbit of normal life. It becomes a question of re-stimulating the human spirit, or what is left of it, of encouraging faith in the future, of drowning the bitterness and hatred of mankind that being a refugee engenders. This is kind of a last chance. We can hardly expect them to have faith in us when they have faith in nothing.

When Don and I and Elena Buonocuore, the savvy U.N. social worker in the camps, selected the first refugees to come to Sardinia, we were always asked the same question: "While the chance for a new life sounds interesting, how can I be sure that if I work hard, I will actually get the fruits of my labor? Will this new promise be empty like all the others?" They wanted to know what the future would be before any future existed. Sometimes after we'd finished all the bureaucratic work to get a refugee out of the camp, at the last minute he would give up,

saying, "I'll stay here. At least I know what I have. Having nothing is more secure than an unknown future."

When the first group of the eventual 15 families arrived at the land we'd bought in Sardinia, there seemed to be an impenetrable barrier that prevented our "getting through." Our basic motivation was suspect: "What's the REAL reason you're helping us? Is it for personal gain?" Our technical abilities were considered more or less worthless. Discussion of economic plans before spending money was complicated because the refugees had had their fill of such proposals, all of which proved empty. We tried to deal with them democratically, not with the absolute authority of the camp director. Rather than spurring cooperation, though, this provided opportunity for them to exploit the slightest little opening; they considered us "suckers" for giving this new freedom. As we learned later, the real intention of some was to "get a quick buck," such as U.N. loans if they agreed to resettle permanently, then take off.

Besides the distrust was a sense of helplessness; they had long since lost the ability to solve problems on their own. The notion had been instilled of the "benefits of refugeedom." The world owed them a living, which increased their inability to take a chance, even if it was offered. Thus, there was the strange dynamic that perpetuated the problem: there was no initiative on the refugees' part to seek a new life, and also there was an entrenched infrastructure of "helpers" (camp employees and agencies) whose jobs continued as long as there was a problem.

Once in Sardinia, we found an interesting attitude in how the refugees related to each other. While in camp they may have cheated and molested each other's women, now there was an unwritten survival code of never speaking against each other to outsiders. Thus, it was difficult to treat them as individuals because they operated as a bloc. When they wanted something, it was a "refugee demand," not an individual request. However, since they differed greatly in education, experience, leadership and cleverness, a few "ring leaders" took charge, just as in camp.

The aggregate of this behavior, characteristic of people who had stagnated for years in camps, was known as the "refugee psychology." A professional with advanced degrees who didn't comprehend this refugee psychology faced a dim prospect of effectiveness. If there was a special attribute of our small group of volunteers working in Sardinia, it was our ability as quick learners to deal with the people we brought from the camps. We won the respect of the U.N. and Italian authorities as few others had done, primarily because we were finding ways to break through the refugee psychology, the key step to independence and self-sufficiency. I was invited to present a paper on "Refugee Attitudes" at a U.N.- sponsored workshop, which later was circulated in U.N. offices around Europe.

I return to Mario, a classic example of the refugee psychology. In the Aversa camp near Naples, he had operated as one of the leaders of the marginal "small businesses." He had resigned himself to life in refugeedom. When Elena Buonocuore, who knew him well, recommended that he join our Sardinia project, she told me: "If you can make it with Mario, despite all the hearsay that you're destined to fail, I'd say that your project has a chance of success."

One of our early acquisitions in Sardinia was a machine to manufacture concrete blocks. This would provide construction materials for refugee homes and provide jobs, both for refugees and local villagers. Since we knew Mario was a "savvy businessman," I made him captain of this block industry. It was heavy work; water had to be hauled from the Tirso River contiguous to our land, then mixed with sand and poured into the machine. Not used to this kind of labor, Mario began to vomit and cough blood. We feared he might not make it. We urged him to take it easy, start up the business gradually. He told us he WANTED to work himself to death. Life had been too hard and it was time to end it all. We pulled him through, and he developed a prosperous enterprise. He married a lovely local woman, and had two healthy children. But all this took a while. Sometimes I'd take him along to visit local officials to see for himself the agencies that were giving us subsidies. He'd never believed this would happen.

The world refugee problem has mushroomed in the intervening years since our Sardinia project half a century ago. There are millions of Marios stagnating in camps in many areas of the world, especially the Middle East and countries in Africa. The U.N. map points out the refugee camps caused by wars, racial and ethnic struggles, and political turmoil. The historic definition of "refugee," established by the U.N and implemented by the High Commissioner for Refugees, describes those who flee their home country because of persecution. But today there are also millions of displaced persons in camps for other reasons, such as natural disasters and economic hardship.

Soon we can expect a whole new category of refugees, already becoming an urgent international problem—namely people facing crises caused by climate change and natural resources calamities. Floods, droughts, desertification, melting of glaciers that feed rivers, rising sea levels and soil erosion are forcing people to leave their homes, sometimes pushing them into temporary camps that become permanent. There is a new terminology replacing the earlier *hard-core*. It's *protracted refugee crisis*.

Protracted refers to "refugees who have lived in exile for more than five years, who cannot go home, cannot settle permanently in their country of asylum, and have little chance of being accepted anywhere." If we accept that many of these people will never be able to emigrate, and will be unable to return to where they came from, the only solution will be to enter the economy in which the camp is located. And the solution, like our Sardinia project in years past, will require rehabilitation to overcome the refugee psychology, and to institute imaginative policies that mesh resettlement with development.

Now, a final comment about Mario, symbolic of countless refugees like him who had spent years in camps. This was the last paragraph of my paper at that U.N.-sponsored workshop on refugee attitudes:

When Mario and another from our project arrived back at the gate of the Aversa camp and saw the usual row of idle refugees sitting on the wall gazing into space, they almost cried out in astonishment: "My God, these people are the living dead! How could they want to stay here?" They entered the camp and many refugees crowded around as though seeing an old friend after a long journey. Now the Sardinia refugees think much as we think but they also know the refugee psychology. As the camp refugees expressed doubts and cynicism about the project, the Sardinia refugees recounted, step-by-step, what had happened. And so came about the dramatic situation of refugees, who not many months before had been too faithless to believe a planted seed would grow, now explaining to others that they, too, could find a new life.

ODYSSEY
Passing Ellis Island: Immigrants or Refugees?
My Father's Family from Norway

by Belden Paulson

B.J. In the early pages of your book, you described how your family arrived from quite different social strata in Europe. As did everyone's who may read this.

Q. Were they "refugees"? Important: how should we look at the issues of immigration involving America today? In fact, this column is scheduled the day after St. Patrick's Day, a celebration of immigration. And, perhaps most important, what about black Americans, who weren't driven out, nor came by choice, but were stolen?

A. My father's parents came from Norway. His mother's family lived on a beautiful farm near Trondheim, which my father and I visited years later. My paternal grandmother, Mari Hansdatter Kulbrandstad, was the only person in her family who dared to leave her home, her family and country, knowing she probably could never return. She obviously thought a wonderful life awaited her in the American land of opportunity. An awakening came when, knowing no English and having no particular training, she settled for being a housemaid for the Pillsbury Flour family in Minneapolis.

Twelve years later she met her husband, my paternal grandfather, John Stav, who had also left the Trondheim area around 1870. Like most Scandinavians in those days, he changed his name—to John Stav Paulson. He was a craftsman and ended up building houses in Minneapolis. I don't know much about these grandparents. Coming from such a spectacular environment in Norway, one would be hard pressed today to figure why anyone would want to leave, but in the latter 1800s Norway was a poor country while America was the magnet of unlimited possibility. When Pop and I visited his cousin in Norway in 1961, we also met her 10-year-old grandson, Oddvar. His wall was already full of sports plaques; later he won two Olympic gold medals for cross country skiing and today is considered a Norwegian icon.

These folks, like millions of others who arrived in our country, and here in Sheboygan County, were immigrants—aliens lawfully admitted to the U.S. for permanent residence and eventual citizenship. The term *refugee*, for a person who flees to another country to escape danger or persecution, became used popularly at the end of WWII when millions of people were displaced. Due to political, racial or religious discrimination, they couldn't return to their homeland. The United Nations established a Convention providing them minimum legal rights as stateless persons until they could find new homes. Unhappily, some didn't find homes—for years, or ever—continuing to exist in camps.

My mother's family goes back to the kings and queens of England, almost a thousand years. The lineage reportedly included signers of the Magna Carta. Some relatives immigrated to America in the 1600s; some, such as William Henry who was born in 1728 and was a gunsmith in George Washington's army, played significant roles in the American Revolution. My grandfather, William Henry Belden, had been a Congregational minister, a graduate of Yale University, with pastorates in the 1880s. His family became ministers, lawyers and teachers, educated in the best colleges. My grandmother, Ellen Henry Scranton, came from a family of regional business leaders, inventors and political figures. My grandfather brought his young wife and first two children to Turkey where he served as a missionary. In those days, at the turn of the century, going abroad as a Christian missionary, was one of the highest callings.

Soon thereafter his health broke down, and after his early death in 1896, my grandmother, now with five small children, left the East where all her relatives lived, for the semi-wilderness of Ohio. She used her husband's insurance money to build a house and raised her five children in the college town of Oberlin. My mother, her four siblings, my sister, and I all attended Oberlin College.

The courtship of my parents was classic Americana. My mother, Evelina Belden, had a distinguished career as a pioneer in the early years of the social work movement. She served with Jane Addams and Graham Taylor in Chicago, joined the U.S. Children's Bureau and was involved in the tense years dealing with civil rights in the South. She operated as an undercover dance partner with a member of the U.S. Secret Service investigating Chicago dance halls for the white slave trade, corrupt police, and narcotics. Just after WW I she directed the American Red Cross social work program in war-ravaged Poland.

My father, Henry Paulson, quit school in Minnesota after the eighth grade to help support his family. He finished high school late and was the first in his family to graduate from college. His major professor recommended that he pursue graduate work in Chicago while working as secretary to a judge. With minimal family support, he struggled to put himself through law school. It turned out that both he and my mother lived at the Chicago Commons social settlement house, first meeting there in 1914. As she was often away traveling, their on-and-off relationship revealed their radically different backgrounds and personalities. Even though my mother's family had little money, they were highly educated, religious, idealistic, world-minded, and provided strong support as her career evolved. Later, she was offered any social work job she wanted in Europe.

My father was also idealistic, helping out in the settlement center's surrounding slum and making astute analyses of the underlying causes. But after a hard life, with virtually no family support, he was more or less alone in the world, was afraid to take risks, and always held a pessimistic view that things would not work out. His stolid stubbornness and independence, perhaps honed from his Norwegian ancestry, caused him to give in to no one, often to his disadvantage. With predecessors of peasant stock, close to the earth, and a penny-pinching autocratic father (although his mother was a saint), and not much interested in religion, he also let my mother know that he had no particular respect for elite family pedigrees or affiliations with prestigious Eastern schools. While my mother was receiving accolades for her work, my father had just lost his first legal case, was living in a cheap boarding house, and was trying to figure out how to make ends meet. Notwithstanding his seeming inability to sell himself in public, he had become a surprisingly adept salesman in their courtship, expressing forthrightly not only his failings but also his integrity and solid strengths, and certainly his love. He was a masterful writer; he wrote her:

> *I want you to think of your own good. I set myself before you as I am. I can't complain should the consequences be not as I'd want them. I shall not whimper. Yet I do love you.*

I doubt that she heard that kind of straight talk among the colleagues and bureaucrats with whom she worked.

In 1922 they married, and although they had their ups and downs, this marriage of opposites was a lasting relationship, producing two kids and four grandchildren, and enjoying many happy moments. He died at the venerable age of 89, eight years after my mother.

In the years while I was writing my memoir, prowling through hundreds of old letters that revealed my family's past and present, I became fascinated with other peoples' roots. As the ancestors of most people of my generation were immigrants from Europe, I was curious as to their origins. Having worked for years with black colleagues in the Milwaukee African American community, their histories (keep in mind that there were four million slaves in the U.S. until the 13th amendment to our Constitution in 1865 ended that horrendous institution) enhanced my current understanding of the importance of background. I've also worked with Native Americans—there are currently almost three million in the country—not knowing at the time that research has found them migrating on a land bridge across what is now the Bering Sea, from Siberia to Alaska, some time between 25,000 and 60,000 years ago. This very long history may relate to the inbred wisdom I associate with indigenous peoples. I thought about the scores of refugees I knew in Italy and elsewhere, many of whom had led dignified, successful lives before they fled from communism or were displaced by war. It seemed the luck of the draw that I was the one born into fortunate circumstances while so many others found themselves incarcerated in barbed-wire camps.

Since our country has been built on immigration, our very future depends on enlightened policy. The U.S. Congress, way back in 1790, began considering how to enable people from abroad to become U.S. citizens. In 1875, a Federal law blocked immigration for criminals and prostitutes. After WW I, when mass immigration began, a policy known as the National Origins Quota System was enacted, favoring reunification of families. Since the end of World War II, a lot of attention has been given to specific groups of refugees, and the Refugee Act of 1980 brought U.S. policy in line with the 1951 U.N. Refugee Convention. In more recent years, there's been increasing interest in how to deal with the more than 10 million illegal migrants in the U.S. This problem could be political dynamite, where long-term needed reforms may clash with short-term electoral concerns. This involves such volatile questions as how to enforce existing laws, and how to structure the preferred path of illegal migrants to become U.S. citizens.

Despite all the controversy related to current immigration policy-making, certain goals have been generally achieved. We now have policies that:

1) favor reuniting families;

2) contribute to our economy and scientific achievements through attracting people with specific skills;

3) provide opportunities for refugees who face persecution in their country of origin;

4) will assure diversity from countries with historically low rates of immigration to the U.S.

This is all a long way from conditions centuries ago when my ancestors made the decision to face the great unknown and to emigrate to America.

Lisa's maternal grandmother (child at bottom front) and family, around 1880

MARCH 23, 2010

ODYSSEY
My Forebears: Heritage for a Non-conventional Outlook

by Lisa Paulson

B.J. Lisa, in the early pages of Belden's autobiography, he described how his forebears arrived at very different times and from different social strata in Europe.

Q. What can you tell us about your parents and your early family life?

A. My father's forebears came from England and Scotland. John Hill (Hill was my maiden name), an ancestor on his father's side who came to resent the social discrimination and political orientation in England, was the earliest to sail to the New World. He and his family landed on the Connecticut coast in 1639, the same year (and maybe on the same boat?) as Bel's, according to our family trees!

Some of the relatives ended up farming in upstate New York.

His maternal great-grandfather was James Scott, who worked in a woolen factory in Huddersfield (Yorkshire), a weaving center from early on. Toward the mid-1800s machines were fast displacing men in the mills, an incentive to migrate to America. Another factor was that he and his wife were shunned and abused when they joined The Teetotalers, a temperance organization generally discredited. They booked passage from Liverpool to New York in 1842, gradually making their way to Wisconsin via canal boat, small sailing vessel, and ox cart. James tried farming and the woolen business across several Midwest states, ending up in Vicksburg, Michigan, where his son William, my father's grandfather, was a dentist—and where my father was born.

His father, Albert, became a gentle English professor at the University of Chicago, and his paternal grandfather was a well-known botanist in the Chicago area. There was a tense time when his mother and younger sister came down with influenza during the great epidemic of World War I and nearly died. When my father was 12, the family moved west where his father was to chair the English department at the University of Nevada. It was not quite a covered-wagon journey, but in 1912 this definitely meant heading into wilderness territory. Even in 1932, when I was four and making my first trip out west, I remember vividly the Indian children leading ponies to hawk rides up and down the dusty dirt streets of Reno. My grandfather became the beloved "Mr. Chips" on campus; one of his students was Walter Van Tillburg Clark who later wrote *The Oxbow Incident* and credited my grandfather with inspiring him to become a writer.

Reno was where my father grew up and where he came to love the mountains and outdoors so deeply, a passion he passed on to me, to my brother and my boys. As a young surveyor in the Sierra Nevadas, he often had to ski and snowshoe to survive in winter. He left home after early graduation from college in Reno to move East, going "on test" as an electrical engineer for General Electric where he worked all his life, being moved numerous times up and down the East Coast.

My mother was Pennsylvania Dutch (technically Pennsylvania German), born and raised in Harrisburg. Her earliest ancestor to emigrate from near Hamburg, Germany, in 1825 was a Dietrich (others were Rupps and Harps). They came to America for religious freedom, and all were active in the United Brethren and Lutheran Reformed churches, "nurtured in piety." They became farmers and tradesmen, settling in both Pennsylvania and Maryland. Mother's father graduated from a small local college (no one else in the family had gone past high school). I was told stories about her grandmother being mistreated by a sadistic stepmother and running away at age 15 to hire out as a maid. My grandfather directed the choir in the church where my grandmother sang; this is where they met. My grandfather became a successful businessman, selling farm implements, and built a substantial home in a new suburb of Harrisburg. My mother, valedictorian of her high school class, decided she needed to escape from her provincial milieu to go to Smith College in Massachusetts. Her parents tried to talk her out of it; why leave Harrisburg? But, stubbornly, she went, where her classmates soon taught her to drop her "uncultured" accent. She became a social worker, taking jobs in the worst areas of New York and Atlantic City, then landed in Schenectady where my father was working. Both lived in separate boarding houses (the norm for the young working crowd), but soon they met at the popular ice-skating parties. I heard about poems recited shyly and then a proposal. They married under the rose arbor of the lovely Harrisburg house and soon moved to New Jersey when Daddy was assigned to the New York office of G.E. He used to talk about those heady early days of the company when the young engineers sometimes slept on the floor of the office (down the hall from the president) when there were serious power outages and the engineers had to be ready to dash out to troubleshoot (one time he had to climb to the tip of the Empire State Building to check a lightning strike).

The longest I ever lived in one place growing up was six formative years in rural Connecticut during World War II. There I raised goats, all the family pitched in to grow a Victory Garden, and we foraged for wild plants and berries. There are memories of my father as an air-raid warden, scanning the night skies for planes that might be communicating with German submarines lurking off the nearby shore; darkening the windows with blankets; my mother forced to learn to ride a bike (no one had gas to drive); she and the neighbors rolling bandages in our living room; the school bus commandeered for commuter transport to the train twelve miles away.

One time I was riding this early morning bus and found myself sitting across from blind and deaf Helen Keller. We chatted through her companion and when I told her I played the cello, she beamed and said: "Oh, the cello is my favorite instrument, like wind in the pines." Another time, our neighbor up the road, the renowned orchestra conductor Fritz Reiner, was delivered by his chauffeur to the bus stop outside our house; while waiting, he heard me practicing and came up to the door to listen and talk. Everybody in town, from famed artists to farmers, grew close, sharing on all levels during this period. The war, terrible as it was, became a remarkable unifying force, and those years are a powerful memory for me.

So I grew up, moving around frequently—from New Jersey to Connecticut, to Buffalo, to Baltimore, to Pittsfield, Mass., and Schenectady. When my father drew a stint back in New York in 1959, my parents finally returned to Connecticut where they had bought a couple of acres; they built the house they would live in for the rest of their lives. My father died at 93 and my mother at 102.

In his fifties, my mother's father suffered a collapse of his business and lost everything, which brought on a devastating stroke that destroyed his mind. My grandmother was reduced to living in one of the worst slums in Harrisburg, with freight trains rattling by and black cinders filling her tiny garden where she tried to nurture a few of her beloved flowers. She patiently took care of my addled grandfather until he died 18 years later, surviving by selling *The Readers' Digest* door-to-door, but she remained very proud, forever a "lady." My parents were always struggling financially and could only help a little. It was during the Great Depression and my father was terrified every day of losing his job, which paid something like $20 a week. I remember the hobos who came begging regularly to our back door and would sit on the step eating the plate of food my mother took out. It wasn't until I was past college that my parents felt they could breathe easily; my father was so scrupulously ethical that even when he came up to making $27,000 a year and was offered a raise, he refused, saying the job wasn't worth more than that. He ended up as chief recruiter of engineers worldwide for G.E. Wherever my parents moved, they immediately plunged into leadership roles in the town—church, politics, every organization doing responsible work. They sought out the intellectual groups and those involved in world affairs. They held to the highest moral standards, though always within the boundaries of mainstream activities and thought—which may explain why I was tempted from an early age to rebel and to deliberately move outside conventional paths. (But that's another story.)

Athos Ricci (left), Bel's research partner in Genazzano

MARCH 30, 2010

ODYSSEY
Athos Ricci, and "A Man in Every Village"

by Belden Paulson

B.J. In your book you tell the story of Athos Ricci and the development of your strategy for "a man in every village."

Q. What relevance does this have for our situation in Afghanistan as well as other parts of the world?

A. After leaving my job resettling refugees in Sardinia, I was hired by the United Nations in Rome to strategize solutions for the remaining refugees in camps all over Italy. While in Rome I became very close to Athos Ricci, who recently had left the Italian Communist Party. He and his brother had played major roles in bringing communism to Genazzano,

a town in the hills south of Rome that had become one of the most communist-voting towns in all of Italy, also known as "Little Moscow." Reportedly, Genazzano was well known in the Kremlin where some of the party's local elders had visited.

Purely by chance I had heard about Athos from the editor of a political journal in Rome who knew about my interest in village communism. He said, "You must visit Genazzano." It was a delightful trek from Rome's sweltering heat to find the evening cool at this higher elevation. As we drove through the vineyards clustered on the hillsides, we could see the outline of the medieval castle still guarding this walled town of several thousand souls. I expected we'd spend a couple of hours with this fellow and then head back.

Before we entered his house, Athos made sure that no one had seen us come in with him, or was within earshot. Then he began to unravel his experiences inside the Party, the trauma of withdrawing, his desire to work to strengthen a constructive alternative to communism—and his treatment almost as an ex-convict by the democratic parties.

Now rabidly anti-communist, Athos still had fire in his eyes and talked as a missionary—quite a contrast to leaders of the other political parties I had met, for whom money and career were the dominant motives. It became clear that one reason people found it almost impossible to leave the Communist Party, once in, was the tremendous courage required. Athos said such a person would be threatened and defamed in every way by the communists, while the other parties wanted nothing to do with him.

A week later I returned to Genazzano and Athos became ever more expansive. He entrusted me with a valuable windfall: a set of 12 booklets used in the Party training schools for leaders and activists. I was so fascinated that I read until well past midnight. The booklets dealt with the communist worldview of man and society, the nature of a capitalist society, war and peace, analysis of problems on the village level, speeches by communist leaders directed to specific audiences such as the youth and farmers. After going through all of this, I wrote to Lisa, who had already left Rome with the kids and returned to America:

I wonder how it could be that we, who are so good at selling cigarettes, cannot get across even a fraction of our point of view to these people. I see many holes in their propaganda on every level—ideology,

facts, concrete policies. But do we have anyone studying all of this? I showed the material to John Baker (a good friend of ours at the American Embassy), who was very interested and surprised at its comprehensiveness and sophistication.

By now my curiosity about the workings of this unique town was really stimulated. The Italians and Russians clearly knew all about Genazzano, but America had never heard of it. I decided that I simply had to learn more, and Athos offered to be my link to this treasure trove of information. He would introduce me to all the major players who were the lifeblood of the village.

Since at that time there were no hotels in the town, I arranged to stay at the Irish Augustinian monastery, called San Pio, located high on a promontory outside the village. This ancient structure, used by the Romans to escape the summer heat, was near the castle presided over by the Prince Colona family. In medieval times the Colonas controlled this entire sub region and had produced several popes. Father Duffner, the affable Irish rector of the monastery, said to me:

Let's make a deal: I'll give you a cell and subsistence at no cost; in return, I want you, in your free time, to meet with the 30 priests here who are studying in Rome, and share with them what you are learning in the village. I don't want them to fan out around the world as teachers and know nothing about communism.

Fair enough.

Over the next several months I got to know intimately the valleys and the hills, mostly on foot, with my ever-present guide, Athos, probably the most astute and informed person in Genazzano. He understood the traditional rural culture based in agriculture and craft skills, which was by nature conservative, yet now struggled for a more prosperous life. He understood the historic weight of poverty and injustice and the other key issues to be addressed in order to bring about real change. He looked for a compromise between the traditional and modern worlds. As we immersed ourselves in the life of the town we uncovered an incredibly rich mosaic of characters. There were the old aristocrats who in pre-war days had owned much of the land and held unrivaled economic and political power, although now were penniless, their land expropriated after World War II. There were the former fascists who took control during Mussolini's two decades, with his Blackshirt bullies and thugs running rampant. There was the middle sector of shopkeepers, surveyors, teachers, craftsmen, bankers, bakers and lawyers, who in earlier years were the critical links between the elite and poor, mostly illiterate masses, and now played an even more important role.

While we spent much time with politicians of all stripes, our most authentic conversations were with the small farmers on the land. We'd go into the countryside just after sunrise where huge cacti and low scrub dotted the landscape, lizards rattling through the dry stubble. Some of the land was very fertile—excellent for vineyards and vegetable gardens. We'd yell for a particular farmer, our voices reverberating through the valley, then find the one-room wooden hut with thatched roof where the farmer was resting from the hot sun. In contrast to the politicians, the abrupt forthrightness of these men of the soil was refreshing. While most called themselves communist, they distrusted politics generally.

In the first years after the communists recruited Athos, he was very effective as Party secretary, a gung-ho organizer and educator. But over time he also evolved into a kind of guru, with a wisdom that emanated from his roots in the village's long history. He found he could no longer stomach the paradoxes between the idealists who sought a better life for the village, and the hard-core leaders of the Communist Party who, contrary to their rhetoric, were mainly interested in power. Since Athos lived at home, I also saw a good bit of his family. His father had served in the elite forces at the front in World War I and had lost a leg. Despite his peg leg, he was a dexterous builder. As a local hero, the fascists couldn't touch him. Athos' older brother, like his father, was a top-notch mason who renovated houses. He had been one of the most courageous Resistance leaders who, over and over, narrowly escaped the clutches of both the Nazis and fascists and was in the forefront at the war's end in bringing communism to Genazzano. Although an idealistic reformer, and despite continuing misgivings, he never left the Party and actually gravitated to its inner circle. Athos, instead, notwithstanding all the hazards of leaving, could no longer take the hypocrisy he saw.

Since various American officials and media people were intrigued by my knowledge of grassroots communism, I was regularly asked about the broader ramifications of my studies and observations. (Keep in mind that this was at the height of the Cold War when communism was on the march in much of the developing world, and Italy itself was threatened by leftist takeover.) What could we learn from examples like Genazzano? A friend back home was pushing me to write an article for the *Readers Digest,* which I did after bouncing my ideas off a number of colleagues at the U.N. and elsewhere. Titled "A Man in Every Village," I envisioned the impact that would be possible if the U.S. and our allies could work with many people like Athos. (The *Digest* thought this was "a great idea" but didn't take the article.)

It was my experience that in many of the Italian villages most of the population was too passive and technically unprepared to take leadership for significant social change, yet usually there was at least one *potentially* capable leader. Although these individuals were discontented and frustrated, they lacked the opportunity to do anything—that is, until someone from the outside discovered them and nurtured their leadership qualities. The communists in Italy were proving adept at playing this outsider role, recruiting and training selected people and forming alliances between outside resources and the local potential leaders.

I was asked: Why do these outsiders have to be communists? Others, too, could play this role. It wouldn't require large sums of money; the key is sensitivity to village dynamics and *real commitment to help the people*. One could envisage a hardheaded strategy for developing local leaders having a major impact not only in villages like Genazzano, but also over time helping to groom a new ruling class for Italy's future generations.

Today the great issue is not grassroots communism in Italy, but forces in other areas of the world that are trying to convince the local populace that *they* are on the side of social change, that *they* are the ones who understand the local community dynamics and are committed to helping the people.

Take Afghanistan, where the Taliban have been working on this grassroots level. While there are very real security issues, is there any opposing faction courageous enough to step forward to identify and train the local leaders? A faction that understands and is committed to deal with the real issues of securing a better life? It's not likely that large sums of money and military power, in themselves, will prevail. I believe that reform-minded agencies in Afghanistan, working with nongovernmental organizations and the U.S. and other governments, could bring tremendous benefits with the strategies I've outlined here.

Lisa hauls water and hay for her goats in Weston, Connecticut during the war

April 1 2010

ODYSSEY
Frugal Ways Passed Down in Our Family

by Lisa Paulson

- I always saw my grandmother, and then my mother, darning sox that came out of the laundry with holes. An "egg" was inserted in the sock and they wove thick thread back and forth and across until the hole was closed.

- We changed only one sheet a week (this was before the era of fitted sheets). We took off the bottom dirty sheet for the wash and reversed the top one, bottom to top, making that the new bottom sheet. A clean one went on the top. Saved wear and tear on sheets and laundry supplies.

- When sheets began to wear thin in the middle, we cut them in half lengthwise and sewed the outsides (with stronger material) together in the center. Hence, a much longer life.

- The collars on men's dress shirts (which were worn daily) were "turned" when they frayed.

- My mother (and grandmother) made all their and my clothes. The sewing machine was always out for repairing rips after washing. Likewise, the large sewing basket was always in evidence, filled with bright spools of thread, needles, thimbles and scissors (pinking and small sheers).

- After the Monday laundry came out of the washing machine, pieces to be starched were separated and put into the kitchen sink with the powdered starch and cold water; then they were spun again in the washer before hanging them out in the yard. This was in the days before no-iron fabrics; basically it was shirts, blouses, pillowcases, napkins (of course we used cloth napkins at all meals, each family member with his or her distinctive napkin ring). Ironing (on Tuesdays) was *de rigueur* and a rigorous chore because everything was ironed.

- My grandmother collected all our discarded woolen clothes to make braided and rag rugs. For years afterward I'd recognize favorite coats and skirts and dresses—familiar and loved long ago—in the woven area rugs we walked on.

- Worn-out clothing was torn up for cleaning rags and all buttons carefully removed and saved in different jars according to color and size. Fine lace (often sewn on dresses and blouses) was cut off to be used again.

- Every precious drop of rendered grease from frying was stored and added to in a cup in the refrigerator; this was especially important during the war when fat was scarce and rationed.

- In spring my mother organized expeditions to gather wild greens: dandelions, fiddleheads, mustard. A favorite way of preparing them was to fry with bacon and vinegar. Then there were neighborhood forays into the fields to hunt wild blueberries and strawberries.

- All our preserves were made at home: beach plum (collected on Cape Cod), crabapple, peach, pineapple, raspberry and strawberry jams; watermelon pickle from the rinds we saved.

- During the war we experimented with a clumsy, primitive drier for vegetables, which took many hours (or days) with dubious success.

- I learned that when cracking eggs, I'd get an extra teaspoon or two of whites by swiping out the shells with my finger. Not as elegant as the one-handed sleight-of-hand method of the fancy cooks, but why waste?

- Paper products that we know today were unheard of back in the 1940s and before. You had a cold and used handkerchiefs that you washed yourself. And well into the 1960s, I'd have considered it a sinful waste (and expense) to use disposable diapers. (I still do.) We took for granted soaking dirty dipes in the pail in the bathroom, then washing them and hanging them out to dry on the line. (When we lived in primitive Sardinia, I scrubbed them in the bathtub by hand and held them up one by one to a little electric heater.)

- Likewise, plastics (foil, plastic wrap and hard containers) didn't come in until after the war. We saved the waxed paper our bread loaves came in, folded it and used it to wrap food or cover china bowls of leftovers in the refrigerator.

- During the war, silk stockings were scarce (silk was needed for parachutes), and this was before synthetics were invented (nylon, polyester, etc.), so we teenage girls sometimes painted our legs with orangey "leg makeup," to look like the real thing.

- There was severe war rationing: sugar, butter, meat, cigarettes, tires, and probably other items I can't recall. And, of course, gasoline was greatly restricted. Because we couldn't drive anywhere, the school bus in rural Weston, Connecticut, was commissioned for an earlier run to the train 12 miles away for commuters (that's where I met and got to talk to Helen Keller, Fritz Reiner, and other local notables). We all rode bikes (a hardship for my mother who had to learn and wobbled uncertainly up and down the road).

- Of course Christmas wrapping paper and ribbons (paper and cloth ribbons) were gathered up after the opening of presents, were ironed and put away to use next year. Christmas cards received were cut up so the parts not written on could be recycled to put on presents for the following season. (I also saved favorite cards within the family that appeared year after year on new gifts under our tree.)

- The last tiny bits of soap from the soap dishes were collected and softened in a glass of hot water so they'd stick together to make a larger cake.

- Telephones were used for long-distance calls only in the direst circumstances because rates were prohibitive. If the phone rang and it was our relative in California, we knew it must mean serious illness or a death. And on the rare occasion when my father would call his parents across the country, he'd turn the egg timer over and when the sands ran out, he'd hang up abruptly; his allotted three minutes on cheaper rates were up. When we lived in Italy in the 1950s, we never called our families in the U.S., but relied on frequent letters; even when Bel and I were separated for seven months when I had hepatitis, we never spoke by phone.

- After church there was always a fresh roast for Sunday dinner; then we ate it cold all through the week. Rarely bought additional meat.

- Everyone did their bit for the War Effort. I raised goats and sold the milk (mostly to my family). My brother raised chickens (and had an agonizing time chopping off their heads). We all pitched in to work in the "Victory Garden" and to hay our 2-acre field. My father was an air raid warden who went out on our country road to scan the night skies for enemy planes that might be coordinating operations with subs lurking along the nearby shores of Long Island Sound. Neighborhood women gathered in our living room to roll bandages for the front lines. And when the sun went down, the blackout regulation demanded that everyone hang dark blankets over the windows.

- There was no stigma about accepting hand-me-down clothes from relatives. I was thrilled to inherit my first tweed suit as a teenager from a more affluent aunt. We also haunted thrift stores when I married; the twin beds from Goodwill our boys grew up with are now, after 50 years, still our guest beds.

- Eating out was always an extremely rare treat. I remember once a year my father took us to the drug store for an ice cream soda, a major occasion. Even now, going out for meals mainly happens for a business meeting or for special occasions.

- Now, with the gas crisis, we're reverting to the kind of consciousness we had during the 1940s; we carpool whenever possible out here in the country, and save up errands to do all in one trip. When I go in to Milwaukee, I map out a route where I may make up to 15 stops.

- An admonishment I heard all my life was to turn off all lights during the daytime; otherwise, I was "burning a hole in the day." I retain the habit of switching off lights at night as soon as I leave a room, even if I expect to come back in a few minutes.

Bel and colleague, Reuben Harpole

April 6, 2010

ODYSSEY
Facing the Crisis of Inner City Poverty and Race

by Belden Paulson

B.J. In the mid-1960s you joined the University of Wisconsin-Milwaukee and became immersed in "one of America's most baffling and urgent needs of that day—the twin problems of cities and race."

You developed a close working relationship with Reuben Harpole, who became perhaps the first black professional in Milwaukee Extension.

Q. *How did that association relate to UW's "urban mission," and where did your joint efforts lead?*

[Given the critical importance of these issues that involve all of Wisconsin, this will be a three-part series.]

A. Although I joined the University of Wisconsin as a professor specializing in international relations, I soon found myself face-to-face with one of America's most complex intractable needs: urban problems and racism.

My first university assignments, along with teaching political science, were to help organize one of our country's first programs to train Peace Corps volunteers, and also to take two trips to Brazil to lay groundwork for a development project in its festering Northeast region. But in the mid-1960s all hell was breaking out in America's cities, including Milwaukee.

An inner city leader, Reuben Harpole, was urged by Milwaukee's former mayor, Frank

Zeidler, to come to the university to seek help. He ended up at my office. Over time, I switched gears, and the two of us, strongly supported by innovative deans, created the university's first department committed to inner city work.

As a black man who grew up in this part of the city, Reuben knew every street. He knew the most violent areas where your life was at risk just walking around. Although he knew the hostility that blacks felt toward authority, he himself had a heart of peace and compassion, always trying to build bridges between the races and classes. He was able to communicate with angry, militant blacks as well as the white power structure. He also had an astute and supportive attorney wife. He and I became recognized as the "Bobbsey Twins," because we were seen so often together in public.

While I felt Milwaukee's poverty in no way compared with the caves and ruins of Naples, where I had worked after the war, or the slums in Brazil, I was aware that Milwaukee was in the top ten of America's poorest cities, where even today one in four lives in poverty. Further, the American urban crisis had its own special dimension—race. With its several-square-mile "inner core" north of downtown, Milwaukee was, and still is, one of America's most racially ghettoized cities. In more recent years, some of the black population has moved to the periphery or the suburbs, but in the 1960s virtually all blacks lived in the inner core. It had all of the economic, social, political, and educational characteristics common to very disadvantaged areas.

As a starting point, Reuben said to me: I'll introduce you to the *real* city.

For several months we prowled around every corner of the poorest, most deteriorated neighborhoods. We talked to ministers and teachers, visited shopkeepers, sat in bars, met youngsters and their parents. Then with the help of community groups, we organized a house-to-house survey of 60 blocks, interviewing every parent or guardian where there were young people aged 12 to 22. In the process we trained 30 volunteers from the area, some of whom later worked with us and also were hired as professional surveyors.

One problem kept surfacing with everyone we talked to: deficient reading skills. Once a kid fell behind a couple of grades, by the time he or she reached junior high, a whole bunch of problems followed: lower academic achievement, absenteeism and tardiness, all sorts of behavioral problems.

With our planning group, we sponsored a summer reading demonstration with 42 kids, in close cooperation with Fulton Junior High School located in the middle of the area. Since these kids had never taken learning seriously, our group went to their homes every morning and literally kicked them out of bed.

Then after the class ended at 11 a.m., we walked with them to the nearby public museum (one of the country's finest), where they had never been, for a lunch donated by a businessman friend of Reuben. Attendance for the seven weeks was almost perfect. A student with one of the lowest scores at the beginning read excerpts of essays at the final Recognition Night, sobbing as she received her award.

Some of the local volunteers who had helped with the survey, often parents themselves, were essential in making the program work. We called them community representatives. Fulton Junior High was so enthusiastic that we next organized a program to improve communication between the school, the student and the family. We arranged for 14 community residents to find representatives on each block in the district—we called them block leaders—to develop a process for contacting every family with children in the school. Their job was to prod the kids and families to support the school, while we were urging the school principal and teachers to bend over backward to establish a compassionate rapport with the families.

Along the way, as the community reps got into the homes, they found high school students who were college material but who were deficient in language skills; they had no idea how to process an application for the university, including for financial aid. We set up programs to deal with these needs, and Reuben got Sears Roebuck to sponsor "Personal Improvement" courses—which became very popular. This whole effort, with minimal cost, was a huge success.

Even though Reuben was a pretty tough guy, sometimes when we walked the streets, I sensed that he, too, felt the increasing militancy and alienation all around us. When he and I sat in his parked car in front of my house in our all-white neighborhood, the police invariably came by and asked what he was doing there. As we know, in the latter 1960s a number of big cities across the country were soon ravaged; Newark, Detroit and Los Angeles were only the worst. From our house three blocks from the university and a mile from the inner city, we could hear sniper fire and incessant police and fire sirens.

Some people thought our country might be ripe for social revolution.

ODYSSEY
Pioneering Groundwork for an Urban Mission

by Belden Paulson

B.J. This is the second column in a series to look at how you became immersed in the problems of inner city Milwaukee in the mid-1960s. You developed a closed working relationship with a black colleague, Reuben Harpole, bringing him into the university to create a new department to deal with the challenges.

Q. What can you tell us about your next steps to meet those dire needs?

A. Our next step was to get inside the structure of the school itself, to work with the teachers. Now we needed endorsement by the central school administration, but that was problematic because there was extreme tension between the community and the school board. Angry inner city leaders were attacking the conservative policy-making and unresponsiveness. There was threat of violence. It took some doing, but Reuben and I sat down with Harold Story, the most influential and most conservative board member, despised by the community and labeled a racist. Finally, he asked: "What do you want me to do?"

We told him we needed authorization for a big project.

Our planning group designed what we called the Central City Teacher Community project. This would involve 15 teachers from Fulton School and 150 families with whom we'd already had contact. Each teacher would commit 20 hours a week for eight weeks in the summer with 10 low-achieving Fulton students, and would receive a stipend and free tuition for a graduate course to improve his/her specialty. They had to figure out how to win the confidence of each kid and motivate the family for learning using any legitimate means—getting into the home, playing ball, going fishing. We also hired, part time, five of our best community representatives to help make contacts and build trust. Our weekly seminar with teachers and community reps ended up with radical thinking about school policy. The teachers also agreed to remain at the school for at least two years, and participate in 10 meetings during the year.

The program proved so successful that Story helped us fund a six-fold expansion the following year with 94 teachers, 900 families, and 18 community reps. The third year it had 200 teachers, 1,500 families, and 40 community reps, reaching a substantial number of inner-city schools. Then we passed it over to the school administration. This high-impact program produced policy results, and attracted national visibility.

Reuben and I had not been working together that long, but our phones now were ringing continuously. He was full of pent-up ideas for projects, and once people learned there was someone at the university who really cared, they had been coming out of the woodwork. We developed a network of 25 tutorial centers, mostly located in church basements, which involved hundreds of kids, and introduced scores of people from churches and commercial enterprises to the urban environment. To harness the talents of many young people we saw being wasted, Reuben used his contacts with the elite high schools to create College Prep/Summer Prep, stimulating their ambition to succeed in education and life.

Leaders in Wisconsin state government told us that existing efforts to employ minorities in decent paying jobs were a disaster. We forged a strategy committee with local company executives to prepare cadres of trainers to encourage "increased sensitivity to the life reality, expectations and behavior" of the company minority work forces. This blossomed into working with the staffs of Milwaukee's largest retail stores, and with federal government agencies such as the Department of Labor and HUD. City and suburban churches contacted us to design similar programs with their congregations.

Although all of this effort was merely a drop in the bucket of huge needs, unknowingly we had a hand in laying the groundwork for an evolving university urban mission. Our work, described in a paper, "Research, Training and Action in Milwaukee's Inner Core," was recognized as the outstanding case study from around the country at the annual meeting of a major professional organization in Chicago. It was an example of how the nation's urban universities must apply "their specialized resources to particular salient problems of the city."

By this time a larger urban crisis was enveloping America. The U.S. government had completed a much-publicized study, "Equality of Educational Opportunity," chaired by Johns Hopkins sociologist James Coleman. It documented the extraordinary racial and ethnic segregation and inequality of educational opportunity in most schools. This soon led to court-mandated decisions to confront racial segregation, including in Milwaukee. And in July 1967, President Lyndon Johnson came out with the "Report of the National Advisory Commission on Civil Disorders." Its ominous conclusion:

> *Our nation is moving toward two societies, one black, one white—separate and unequal . . . Discrimination and segregation have long permeated much of American life; they now threaten the future of every American. . . . To pursue our present course will involve the continuing polarization of the American community and, ultimately, the destruction of basic democratic values. The alternative is not blind repression or capitulation to lawlessness. It is the realization of common opportunities for all within a single society.*

ODYSSEY
Inner City Grassroots /University Partnership

by Belden Paulson

Q. Continuing with the story of how your partnership with Reuben Harpole led to a new "urban mission" for the university, what happened next?

A. Prior to 1968 the Catholic Archdiocese of Milwaukee had supported a number of inner-city schools, but financial problems caused a cutoff of funds. A small nucleus of people created seven Community Schools, the first being the Harambee Community School, in the St. Elizabeth Parish area—the very place where Reuben and I first began working together. When several board members came to us to help them find money, this triggered discussions far broader than finance. If this were truly a *community* school, then the community had to empower itself to support this institution. It had to play a much greater role in deciding what would happen to this area and its people. It was time for a new era of Harambee—Swahili for "Let's Pull Together"—to re-create a beautiful community. It was the same kind of challenge being raised across America.

Reuben and I, also enlisting others in my newly created university department, talked with the Harambee school leaders about the idea of a comprehensive development plan, beginning in a 12-square-block area around the school; this later expanded to 160 blocks.

The purpose was not only to generate support for the school, but to challenge all the prevailing negative trends. We landed several small grants to found the Harambee Revitalization Project (HRP), but had not yet envisaged the project's larger ramifications that were to take place over the next decade. In fact, this revitalization effort is still going on after almost 40 years.

HRP set up a policy board that pulled in forces from around the community; Reuben was the first director, but this changed many times. Over time a small staff was in place, establishing task forces that mobilized local people and official agencies in four sectors: economic development, environment, education, and health and human services. A Harambee Blueprint summarized data from the task forces.

At the end of the 1960s, Congress passed the Omnibus Housing Act and subsequently the Urban Growth and New Community Act, to encourage private developers, cooperating with government, to plan new cities from scratch. At the same time they would be revitalizing old cities; in effect, it would be new towns-in-town. HUD gave Harambee a small grant to envisage its work as a "new town."

One of the visionaries of the national new towns movement, James Rouse, wrote:

We aren't coming up with the right answers because we aren't asking the right questions at the outset . . . What is the purpose of the community? I believe that the ultimate test of civilization is whether or not it contributes to the improvement of mankind.

Rouse founded one of America's most successful new towns: Columbia, in Maryland. Our dean was so taken with the new towns vision that I worked with him and others in the university to plan a Center for the Study and Development of New Communities, a national initiative to be based in Milwaukee. Unhappily, a great proposal was never funded.

While this Harambee effort was one of the hot new initiatives in the university's burgeoning urban mission work, the powers-that-be soon started to raise questions: "These are good ideas but where are the results? Harambee is going nowhere, there are lots of meetings, but we see nothing practical." The authorities, including the Wisconsin Legislature, wanted quick and tangible outcomes for one of our country's most intractable problems. However, significant projects were beginning to emerge.

I taught a UWM political science class with Alderman Ben Johnson, then president of the Milwaukee City Council, who represented the Harambee area. Some class participants who came from the community complained about one block where there were lots full of tall grass, weeds, and an old garage infested with rats—a hideout for delinquents and drug dealers. They asked, Why doesn't the city clean up this eyesore? I asked if anyone had described the problem to their alderman (Johnson), and communicated with the Department of Public Works to clean up the garbage. No one had a clue as to how to go about it.

Using the blackboard, I described how the political system was supposed to work: the relationship between inputs (demands on the power structure) and outputs (getting results). Merely being upset usually accomplished nothing. They had to organize, communicate with the appropriate authorities, explain the problem clearly. (Ben Johnson gave clear procedural details.) We then invited for discussion the county supervisor for county problems and a school board member for that jurisdiction.

Agnes Cobbs was one of our first, and one of the best, of our community representatives. Now she became a staff member in my department, working with Reuben and me to create the Political Base Project. The goal: to educate the community to build a strong block organization, using the model discussed earlier. In due course Agnes nurtured over 200 trained leaders; they understood how to identify needs and process them through the system. Called the Harambee Ombudsman Project, this brought results, seen by political officials regularly attending its meetings. It became a model for the city and was known nationally.

As the block captains, in touch with every family in their blocks, began identifying housing needs, the HRP established the Harambee Development Corporation. This nonprofit community development corporation raised funds for a comprehensive home maintenance program, which later expanded into dealing with home insulation, energy audits, and working with housing authorities on zoning violations and vacant lots. The block leaders also identified health and human services problems, which eventually led to establishment of a community health clinic offering comprehensive services, as well as an array of efforts to improve delivery of human services, given that one-third of residents received some form of public assistance.

The new town-in-town thinking stimulated creative thinking about the purpose of all this effort. It was agreed that the goal was to build a healthy community. We conceptualized the meaning of *health* in four dimensions: economic, educational, environmental, and political. My colleagues and I scoured the university to find qualified thinkers to work with us on defining these operationally, and to develop yardsticks to measure progress. Our team held seminars that mixed the university faculty and grad students with people drawn from the community. Everyone found this an exciting intellectual exercise, and with practical community benefit.

This Harambee program was only one of the many efforts in which Reuben and I and our university colleagues invested major energy. Its effectiveness illustrated a number of essential factors: a close working relationship between university resources and community participants where there is learning from both sides, and successes and failures are shared; the need for radical thinking, such as the new town-in-town idea and the redefinition of "health"; a comprehensive approach that brings in many different disciplines and skills; and the willingness for long-term commitment given the complexity of urban problems.

These elements were detailed in a monograph my colleague Dan Folkman and I offered at national meetings. Titled "A Reporting and Planning Model for Urban Community Development," we used Harambee as a case study, showing how educational institutions can work with poor urban communities on complex problems, from formulating the seed ideas of projects all the way through to achieving goals while utilizing the resources of both.

Bel with block leader Agnes Cobbs

April 20, 2010

ODYSSEY
Extraordinary Inner City Women
Don't Take "No" for an Answer

by Belden Paulson

Q. You write about the dynamism and persistence of Agnes Cobbs in your inner-city work. Could you describe the role she played?

A. Agnes Cobbs was one of the very significant figures in our urban work. Short and unassuming, the idealism of this black woman was so radiant that it quickly won over everyone. She became a community force.

When we organized the network of more than 20 tutorial centers through my university urban department that were scattered throughout Milwaukee's Harambee area, one of the most effective ones was located at the Mount Moriah Baptist Church in the heart of the inner city. The minister, Reverend Kenneth Bowen, said: "If you get Agnes to coordinate the center, I'll guarantee it will be one of the best."

He was right. Over several years this network—with her center out front—became the model for how to do it.

With the UWM School of Education's Reading Clinic, we published a 50-page booklet, utilized citywide and beyond, that became the operational manual. Titled *Problems, Pitfalls and Prescriptions for Organizing Volunteer Reading Tutoring Programs,* our dean wrote in the Introduction:

What heights could be reached if we were to design an institutional structure that helped everyone to the maximum of his ability? What would be the economic gain to this country if those who are poorly educated were better prepared . . . [This] is a sincere effort to offer greater hope and unlock some of those miracles.

The community people we enlisted, working as volunteers, started out to conduct surveys. Once we realized the huge importance of reading, we organized these centers, usually based in churches. The key was the coordinator: someone who lived in the area, knew the community and the kids who needed help, could work with and be respected by the schools, was able to recruit other local volunteers as tutors, could work with others drawn in from around the city, and could learn from and cooperate with the university reading clinic. We got a grant to pay the coordinators a small stipend.

These folks were part of the key group we called "community representatives." In their liaison role, both with the community and the university, they took on a certain status; they became known as energetic workers of high integrity who really cared about meeting community needs. They soon served as the heart of the series of programs we developed to improve communication between the community and public schools—the Central City Teacher-Community Project—which was to include many schools in Milwaukee's inner core. They became the forerunners of a new category of public school staff: the teacher aide.

Most of them were women, and frequently they were active church members. It was obvious that in the inner city, in most instances it was the woman who held

the family together, and the church was the central community institution people could turn to.

I talked our dean into financing positions for two of our most effective community representatives, Agnes Cobbs and Mary Suttle. They both joined my new urban department, the Center for Urban Community Development (CUCD). Along with Reuben Harpole, they were among the first professional staff hired by University Extension from the minority community. Mary soon resigned due to illness, but over the next 20-plus years Agnes distinguished herself as one of the university's most prominent representatives from the minority community. Like Reuben, she won many awards.

Agnes, assisted by a bright graduate law student, Todd Honeyager, played the lead role in organizing our block work organization, the Harambee Ombudsman Project. Their 200 trained block leaders, most of whom had taken political science courses with me, became adept in getting government agencies to solve problems in this disadvantaged community. Whether on the blocks or in government, people had a hard time saying "no" to Agnes.

She gathered around her a nucleus of dedicated assistants; if I had space, I'd mention every one. For example, Ethel McGrew occupied the cover of the *Milwaukee Journal* Sunday edition in June 1977, and was featured in an article on Block Power. They called this 75-year-old dynamo "the major." When she gave an order, people jumped. She told the neighbors to call her—whenever. "I tell them my phone's right by my bed, and I don't mind being called at any hour."

This block power even related to the university bureaucracy. In one of the periods of stark budget slashing, a university executive informed me that our department was slated for a significant cut, which would drastically affect our inner-city work. After my colleagues Reuben, Dan Folkman, and I discussed this with Agnes, Todd, and some of the block leaders, they urged me to write a letter to the chancellor to inform him that 50 block leaders from Milwaukee's inner city were planning to come to his office in Madison for a visit. They wanted details about the budget and the university's commitment to urban poverty.

I doubted that such a group had ever circulated in the halls of the chancellor's building, least of all 50 vocal black women from Milwaukee's inner city who had learned not to take "no" for an answer. That visit never took place, and our budget was not cut.

ODYSSEY
Northeast Brazil—Entrenched Oldstyle Politics

by Belden Paulson

B.J. In the latter 1960s you were awarded a prestigious social science grant to do research in the northeast region of Brazil, basing at a local university. Working closely with Brazilian faculty and students, the intention was to contribute to efforts underway to improve the wretched conditions there.

You soon found intense anti-American ferment, and tumultuous changes taking place in Brazilian universities. You wrote home:

> *Had I sat in my political science office at UWM conjuring up the most outlandish situation possible in Northeast Brazil, where I would experience, first-hand, what is really going on here, I could not have imagined the experience we're going through now.*

Q. What was it like to function in that kind of environment? How could Americans serve needs overseas when there was an atmosphere of intense suspicion and even hostility?

A. While I'd collected my share of memorable adventures when working in the caves of Naples, resettling hard-core refugees in Sardinia, serving with the U.N., and pursuing community development work in inner-city Milwaukee, I'd never been labeled a spy. In Brazil I was accused of conducting espionage for the CIA. Publicly denounced on the floor of the legislature, and even referred to as "008" (a mini-successor to James Bond), pushed my adventure quotient to new heights.

Northeast Brazil is a huge region with 23 million people, sometimes called the "largest country" of South America apart from Brazil itself. Geographically it's the closest point on the continent to Europe and Africa, settled by the Portuguese in the 1500s. The flourishing slave trade provided cheap, abundant labor for development of large sugar plantations, with power concentrated in the mansions of the Portuguese planters.

When we arrived, that longstanding rigid social order was in a state of siege, with ferment mounting. We were told that half of the 800,000 people in Recife, the region's biggest city, lived in slums, and that a few big sugar barons controlled half the wealth of Pernambuco, the largest and most important state. All the talk was about impending political revolt, some led by radical Catholic priests with the Peasant Leagues.

Since this was at the height of the Cold War, when the American government was increasingly concerned about this restive place on its own doorstep, the U.S. had organized a new development program, the Alliance for Progress. I had already taken trips to Brazil and found great interest there in collaborating with the University of Wisconsin. On a prior summer research expedition to the Northeast, with funds from the Alliance administered by our university, I had made a surprising finding. While studying one small town centered in a large rural area located in the heart of the region's appalling drought terrain, we found an astonishing situation.

Ten years earlier the Brazilian anti-drought agency, DNOCS, had constructed a dam that created a sizable reservoir, which authorities estimated could irrigate some 30,000 acres of valley land. There was potential for transforming this area of extreme poverty into a thriving economy. There could be intensive truck farming, fruit orchards, livestock, and potential for hydroelectric power for small industries. Yet almost *nothing* had been done; the water was evaporating under the hot sun. When I flew across the whole Northeast region, I spotted other dams and reservoirs that were also, strangely, not being utilized. Why?

Cooperating with the Anthropology Institute of the University of Ceará and the local extension agent, I was given seven research assistants. Our project was to administer a questionnaire to a random sample of people, both in the town and in the rural area, as well as designing a "leader questionnaire" for 21 people in different positions of influence. What we found was that the state deputy who represented the area in the legislature, along with his brother, and the vice-mayor, and tax collector in the town more or less controlled all the local political life.

Their policy was to discourage fundamental changes in the economic and social organization of the community, but just to make some small gesture to combat the most acute local misery. The deputy got funds to create temporary jobs, distributed food (using U.S. surplus), and provided minimal medical facilities. But he discouraged *real reforms* such as redistributing land, training for specialized jobs, constructing a high school and, most important, preparing a leadership class with the technical skills and initiative to organize and run an efficient irrigation system. This could transform the area, but it could also jeopardize his traditional leadership.

This story could be multiplied through much of the Northeast—where one could question why those dammed-up reservoirs continued to evaporate, and why American assistance often ended up supporting the status quo, such as entrenching the power of the state deputy and his allies. It was a no-brainer that people in the region were anti-American. I wrote this up in a 58-page publication that was widely circulated: *Local Political Patterns in Northeast Brazil: A Community Case Study*. We were asked by Brazilian reformers to undertake more such studies.

The opportunity for such a study came four years later when I received a Social Science Research grant for further research in the Northeast. My family and I would move to Brazil for one year. Professor Luis Fontenelle, now director of the Institute of Anthropology at the University of Ceará where I had previously based, invited me back; he had recently returned from a semester of teaching at UWM. This institute was the center of social science research in the university and was considered one of the best in the Northeast. As local collaborators, I was given his excellent chief faculty associate, Paolo Elpidio de Menezes, and seven graduate students. I soon found that the political affiliations of these students ranged from strongly conservative right wing, to radical left (actually, *left* of the communists).

I should mention that the smartest and by far most radical student was Wanda. At the outset I felt she didn't trust me, assuming that I was an agent of the Embassy or CIA, but Fontenelle vouched for me. Later, she found me actually more "revolutionary" than her Maoist friends, "who only argue and repeat old stereotypes without ever verifying them." She told me she wanted "to identify the facts, get hold of reality as a basis for serious development."

Fontenelle and his associates decided with me that a very useful project, which had never been attempted before, would be to study the leadership class of the entire state of Ceará. We'd focus on the six major sub-regions and local areas where the future economy could be built. We identified key people, and also interviewed a sample of officials elected to the state and national legislatures. I conducted a political science seminar for his staff and the students, and we invested considerable effort in formulating questionnaires and training for administering them.

Paolo and I tried to set an example for the students by riding the buses—the only public transportation—for long hours to every corner of the state, often on almost non-existent roads. We stopped in towns seldom seen by tourists, slept in small hotels in hammocks with assorted wildlife dive-bombing us all night. Every small town had a large television screen set up in the public square, the main source of news.

We saw whole towns without electricity or running water. We encountered families breaking up as the youth packed their possessions in a sheet to leave the isolation of their mud huts, heading to cities to hunt for work.

I was impressed at how well our group was doing, getting people to talk, rigorously keeping logs of what they were finding. We were appalled at the lack of basic data. Various officials wanted to loan us more workers so we would train them. We collected reams of information. Some of our fascinating adventures are detailed in my *Odyssey* book. But the big adventure began when our research project was attacked in *Ultima Hora*, with the largest circulation in the country for a daily newspaper of the left, published in Rio de Janeiro.

The first paragraph of this front-page story read:

> *The Federal University of Ceará is furnishing all the material necessary for Professor Belden Paulson—of the University of Chicago and the Department of Political Science at the University of Wisconsin—to study and make a collection of socioeconomic, political and cultural material . . . the results of which Brazilians will not have access. . . . It is an investigation without limits. . . .*

My next article will describe the tense but almost comic unfoldment of these bizarre accusations.

APRIL 29, 2010

ODYSSEY
"008": Was an American Researcher in Brazil Really a Spy?

by Belden Paulson

B.J. With a Social Science Research grant in hand for political and economic research in the northeast region of Brazil, you landed in the city of Fortaleza and set up a grassroots research project with Brazilian colleagues.

Q. What happened as you began to dig into the corrupt economic and political system perpetuated in many of the towns of Northeast Brazil where you and your colleagues traveled?

A. The article published in the leftist national newspaper, *Ultima Hora*, was soon taken up by *Jornal Do Brasil*, one of Brazil's most important papers, and then transmitted around the world. Local students now approached Fontenelle demanding that our political-economic research project in the state of Ceará be terminated and that "the North American professor be asked to leave Ceará." Several days later Fontenelle and Paolo Elpidio, with the "right to reply," wrote a second article for *Ultima Hora*, "The research project on 'Political Behavior in Ceará' under our coordination is a program of essentially Brazilian investigations, executed and directed by Brazilians. . . ." For the next months, until my family and I left Brazil, an intermittent battle was waged between the forces that defended the research as a genuine scientific program to benefit Brazil, and those who attacked it with overtones of espionage.

A few highlights included: denunciation and defense of the project in the state legislature; denunciation by a deputy in the federal congress in the capital, Brasilia; suspension of funds of one development agency that wanted to help us; appointment by the University of Ceará rector of two different commissions of inquiry; confiscation by Brazilian customs of some of my materials and books when I left Brazil; ample coverage in local newspapers and radio transmission around Europe, including Radio Moscow. An agent of the inquiry commission even sliced up my tennis balls to "look for messages" being sent to the CIA or State Department. He also examined used toilet paper at my office (deposited in waste baskets but never flushed due to poor plumbing). For a time I was perhaps the best-known North American in Northeast Brazil. A few referred to me as the successor to James Bond. What better "cover" for espionage than a university professor doing research?

As time passed, the details about me and the research got lost in the swirl of a far more significant battle. There was a huge struggle over the future of the University of Ceará itself. Brazilian higher education was in the process of major reform. As various subject areas were being restructured into new departments and schools, there was intense jockeying to determine the designated location of particular disciplines, courses and professors. At the university of Ceará the "hot growth area" for the future was the social sciences; this was highly popular with the students, but there were few courses offered. A new faculty of social sciences was to be created and a dean appointed, with Fontenelle the likely candidate. There was major conflict between the more traditional and more change-oriented faculty and administrators. My presence and research sharpened the debate: was this one more example of "Yankee penetration"? Was political science research a foreign subject of no particular value? Or, was this the kind of scientific enterprise that deepened understanding of the state's social realities that could lead to development strategies, including training and international collaboration?

Eventually the inquiry commissions gave up, having found nothing. There was a time when Fontenelle and his bloc threatened "to call out the students into the streets." He and others kept a pistol handy in their desks "just in case." I was warned that "anything could happen." The social sciences, including political science, were attracting new intellectual interest, and Fontenelle, whatever people thought of him personally, was gaining new visibility and respect as an articulate voice for change, not to mention as the staunch defender of a North American project.

My student, Wanda, faced a dilemma: all of her peers were pushing her to denounce our research, but she ferociously allied with the "change" bloc. At a critical moment, in the face of the opposition, she stood up publicly in the streets, risking her own neck to defend me. She wrote in her final report: "it was my first objective and systematic experience in the field of social science. . . . It was much broader, opening up economic, sociological and anthropological aspects of political relationships, and the distribution of power. This experience showed me the possibilities of rigorous and scientific work; we could define the types of forces that determine why some people govern and others are governed, and of the possibility for people themselves to become determiners of their fate rather than be determined by others. It gives scientific understanding about the kind of political system that could be an instrument for effective participation in a transforming society."

I helped two of the Institute faculty to come to UWM for graduate degrees, although, regrettably, nothing worked out for Wanda. Paolo Elpidio later became the rector (head) of the University of Ceará, and visited UWM to sign an agreement for cooperation. On returning home, I presented a paper at a professional meeting of Latin Americanists, "The Role of the North American Political Scientist in a Foreign Area of Social Change. . ." I emphasized the importance of a partnership relationship based on equality, not domination; of recognizing that instability and anti-Americanism are likely ingredients of the change process; that personal relationships are extremely important, and that some knowledge of the language and culture is essential. I said that our professed commitment to democracy and freedom would probably breed disorder and some chaos in the short run, and that the human dimensions of American culture tend to shine through far more than the financial and military.

I concluded that the "window of opportunity" in areas of rapid change is narrow and requires extreme sensitivity. And that despite the steep challenges, there is a useful and needed role for Americans in places of suspicion and even overt hostility.

ODYSSEY
An American Family Is an Island in an Alien Ocean

by Lisa Paulson

Last week Bel wrote about his adventures as a so-called "CIA spy" (erroneously labeled in the Brazilian press). To us it seemed a somewhat humorous, if inconvenient, flap. This was Bel's third investigatory trip from the University of Wisconsin to the Northeast of this vast country—to explore reasons why the local political infrastructure refused to make use of a number of large reservoirs that could have turned around the terrible drought/starvation situation in this dust bowl region. This time, in the fall of 1967, our entire family moved to Brazil for a year. While he has explained how his academic research was interrupted by widespread suspicion of any North American—and actual accusations of espionage by left-wing factions— our family of four (our two sons, Eric and Steve, were 11 and 7) was experiencing another set of interesting challenges in this frontier culture located slightly south of the equator.

A Brazilian medical doctor on leave in the U.S. had agreed to rent us his house in Fortaleza, a fair-sized city with a sprawl of mostly one-story buildings—modern homes interspersed with tin shacks of the very poor. As our plane swooped down, we were struck by the vast expanses of white sand fronting the Atlantic Ocean, a magnificent magnet that was to draw us to the beaches almost

daily. (The temperature remained the same year round—into the high 80s—though the Brazilian winter also brought brief daily showers, and darkness started setting in by 3:30 p.m. when it became too cool to swim.)

Because our house had sat empty for several months, vandals had climbed in the windows and carried off almost all the furniture we had been promised. Thus commenced our "camping" adventure. For much of the next three months, there was no water and we hauled buckets from one small faucet in the garden. There was no electricity: all the sockets shot flames and the ceiling fixtures crackled and spit fire with every gust of wind. When the water finally did come on, it was disconcerting to discover that the contents of the toilet, when flushed, whooshed by under the shower and sat there 2 inches below broken tiles. We had trustingly assumed that eventually sewage was carried off to sea or wherever, but alas—each house had a pit dug beneath and when this overflowed, people just dug another. When our toilet failed completely, Pedro, our outdoor helper, simply tossed it out of the upstairs window and buried it neatly in the garden.

Speaking of water, assuring a safe supply that was not deadly was quite a process: first, we poured tap water into a clay filter where, over a 48-hour period, the "big stuff" was captured; then we boiled the water for 40 minutes by the clock, and finally could drink it (and cook with it). All this took a certain amount of planning so we wouldn't run out. There was no bottled water. In the same vein, fresh vegetables were considered unsafe, partly because they were often grown with human fertilizer that might be contaminated with parasites. We carefully washed our lettuce in Chlorox (no, the taste didn't persist!).

More on parasites—we couldn't go barefoot outside for fear of contracting schistosomiasis from worms in the soil, an affliction that left people listless for life.

The boys were especially delighted with the exotic wildlife. The most pleasant visitors were small lizards that zipped over the walls and ceilings like lightning. There were magnificent 4-inch flying cockroaches with a special affinity for the breadbox in the kitchen and the shower and our damp toothbrushes. One of them, "Archibald," resided all year inside Bel's typewriter. Ants appeared in troops when the signal went out that a feast was in the offing; the walls became black with them, but magically they were gone by morning. I even found a swarm of tiny ants in our bed. Then there were the bats. Every time we left a door or window open at night (screens were unheard of in Brazil—they would cut off welcome breezes), we'd hear the bats chattering and one would swoop in and dart all over the house. One night we were busy herding some aggressive cockroaches out the front door while Steve was shrieking, "Quick, shut it before the bat comes in!" Another day a seven-inch tarantula appeared on the kitchen ceiling, sitting harmlessly enough, but Bel felt it should be dispatched.

There was no sign of regulatory devices such as calendars and clocks around the city,

but there must have been some primitive mystique that enabled certain rituals to occur with frightening punctuality. Here was a typical morning: By 5 a.m. the Early Symphony was well under way and swelling to a grand contrapuntal crescendo. Neighborhood canines had been vocal most of the night, but an abundance of roosters were poised to announce the rising sun (at 4:30). Next door, a black lamb complained continually, adding to the chorus. Across the street, wandering among ornate fountains and tropical foliage was a princely billy goat who responded hoarsely to the plebeian bleats of his kin. Next, a procession of squeaking, creaking two-wheeled carts (with auto tires) jounced over the cobblestones, the drivers whipping their donkeys into vocal protest as they jockeyed for first crack at the customers with a bit of produce from the country. Barefoot boys loped past hawking giant red snappers carried on sticks across their shoulders where only the remembrance of shirts flapped in faded strips. At 7:10 sharp, the garbage truck bore down, its "sanitary engineers" screaming warnings to all who might have forgotten to leave their cans at the curb. In a flash, the crew leaped down, flung the refuse with its normal quota of ants onto the heap and rumbled around the corner. At precisely the same moment, the cry *correio!* boomed and we had to rush to the gate to snatch letters the mailman had balanced in the grillwork, the next instant to be whirled off in the perpetual seaborne gusts if not retrieved.

An assortment of vendors, beggars and would-be maids passed the house continually. Instead of doorbells, they used the Chinese custom of clapping outside the gates. Although our Portuguese was passable when we arrived, we still needed help to maneuver around the intricacies of the local systems, including bargaining at the vegetable market and operating the household. We found Maria, a handsome young Indian woman from the dry interior area who was totally illiterate. Her pay was $12 a month, generous by local standards. Because of her own roots in stark poverty, her heart went out to the parade of mothers who came to our gate trying to give away their ragged children so they, at least, might escape inevitable starvation.

I remember especially one gaunt, barefoot mother with a little girl about six years old who was screaming and trying to run away. Maria got the story: the woman's husband had died and left her with six small kids in the interior without support. So she had undertaken the long trek—days—on foot with the whole brood, carrying two little paralytic boys. She told how they had all slept in the street the night before and gotten soaked in a downpour. None had eaten since the previous morning. She had left all but this one rather pretty girl sitting on a curb across the city some five miles away. Now, in desperation she was scrounging the better neighborhoods for a bit of food, and was literally attempting to give the children away. She offered this one to Maria to bring up: "She won't get in the way or make trouble; if you could just give her a little milk and bread in the morning and once in a while a little dress—please, please!" We could only send her away with a small package of food.

The sixth member of the household was Mishki, a pup donated by our neighbor, the Peace Corps director. People told us it was good to have a watchdog, though we felt safer than most because the commanding general for the entire region lived next door. The moon would glance off two helmets and bayonet-rifles as guards sauntered up and down all night. Eight more guards were parked inside the house with sub-machine guns. Down the road, leaning their kitchen chairs against the governor's pink wall, were three soldiers. Despite such military displays and talk of ferment (mainly in American magazines), revolution seemed a long way from Fortaleza. Life continued as it had for decades, as far as we could tell—the very rich living it up and taking advantage of the poor who were too used to subservience to object.

Our boys adapted well. They walked to an English-speaking school run by Baptist missionaries. We might have preferred a Brazilian one, but the local school year began in March, which proved too confusing. The teaching was excellent, though, and six to a class would have been hard to beat. With such numbers, extras were possible: trips to the mountains, going to a bowling alley with the teacher, a baseball game with the players all riding donkeys. But our greatest love was the sea. Eric and Steve became absolutely fearless, rushing to meet a 15 to 20-foot wave. They dove through them, rode in with them on boogie boards, or were smashed down by them, all with equal delight. At home the craze was family Canasta, an evening ritual as sacred as Kennedy touch football, accompanied by roasted cashews, and rum and coke (for Bel and me). Of course there was no radio or television. Some evenings (always warm and breezy), we'd explore the innumerable little cobbled streets near us, peeking into lavish gardens to watch Brazilian night life on the wide terraces and verandas (some very wealthy families might have modest furnishings inside because all entertaining was in the garden).

Here's the scene on one such ramble: orchids climb the trunks of coconut palms, colored lights wink from tall branches into tiny reflecting pools. On the sidewalks, scores of hula-hoops twirl on gyrating youngsters (did it take 10 years for this U.S. fad to reach Northeast Brazil?). Wild West hoof beats ring out down the block and a lone horseman gallops past, making us dive for the gutter. A majestic Brahma bull swaggers by, three small boys squeezed behind his hump. Four unattended donkeys reach a busy intersection and amble nonchalantly across, the stream of cars swerving expertly but not slowing. The maids from nearly every house are leaning over the gates gossiping or are wrapped in the arms of their *namorados* against a wall. A Ford Galaxy pulls up behind a line of other Galaxies and Impalas (both produced in São Paolo) and discharges four robust ladies with monumental hairdos, brocade gowns and gold slippers. They disappear up an elegant walk flanked by dark mango trees, but not before an appalling creature has materialized from the pavement, crawling crab-like on all fours, except belly upward; the harsh street lamp catches his sucked-in brown cheeks, grimy rags and worn, bare feet (or are they hands?—they look the same). He tells the matrons he will guard their car. . . .

Having lived abroad before (in Italy), we grew to treasure this enforced family togetherness, sadly lacking most of the time at home where everybody scatters for separate activities (now, of course, even more than 40 years ago, as they disappear into their electronic devices). In Brazil, the four of us drew together naturally, a little island suspended amidst an alien ocean. We delighted in making our own fun, planning outings and explorations. It was a way of life that we all look back on now as having been particularly happy, exciting and meaningful.

Fishermen drag their jangada out of the surf; they sail for up to a week at sea on this raft

MAY 11 2010

ODYSSEY
Life in a Land of Contrasts

by Lisa Paulson

I've described the arrival of our family of four into Northeast Brazil for a year while Bel pursued political research in the outlying areas of the state of Ceará. Our initiation into this very different culture made for constant eye-opening adventures that pointed up the tragic, dangerous results of vast economic and social discrepancies. We found some things that were hard to condone, but at the same time there was much to love and savor about this beautiful, "frontier" country.

A word about the three people employed by us.

Maria, in her mid-20s, lived in and turned out to be a remarkably able, intelligent and enjoyable person to have around—my constant companion and teacher of local customs. At Christmas I upped her salary to $13 a month, almost twice what she had ever made before. I had to push her to take Sundays off. Like thousands of others, her beginnings were rough. She grew up in the interior *sertão* with 15 brothers and sisters. Her mother died when she was nine, and she had to start working full time in the blistering fields from then on, picking beans, rice and cotton. The almost non-existent wage she earned was turned over to her father and she even had to forage for her own clothes. Her mother had been a dressmaker, and Maria's considerable skill was absorbed after watching her mother.

Then her father sold the sewing machine and Maria would practice by cutting out paper dresses for her doll; she never had real material. None of the children were allowed to go to school; they were sent to the fields. In the year of the great drought, 1958, she traveled alone and terrified to Fortaleza (she was 15), and hired out as a maid. Her ambition all along was to buy a sewing machine and begin to earn as a seamstress. Finally, after moving in with us, she worked out a deal to get a secondhand pedal type, paying half down from what she'd saved and the rest from future salary. We planned to drive together in the jeep to get it, a momentous occasion.

Didiza, a girl of about 20, came once a week to wash and iron (on a scrub board with bars of soap). She had two small daughters and no husband. Like a large percentage of the slum dwellers, she married young, but was abandoned as soon as the children got to be a burden (i.e. as soon as they were weaned). She lived in one of many favelas ringing the city, in a tiny mud shack on land donated by the prefecture (which could be taken back for some building project). When Maria rescued some large palm fronds pruned from the general's garden next door, Didiza was overjoyed and came to get them with a donkey cart to build a roof over the tin charcoal stove that was her kitchen.

Pedro was the third member of the team, a young man in his 20s who came every other afternoon. A near genius, he fixed everything from electrical connections to serious plumbing defects. He built tables and gates, constructed window screens (for two bedrooms), washed the car and dog, waxed the marble floors and painted the walls. He dreamed up a weird sprinkler system for the garden,

watered the hibiscus and rubber plants, tended the coconut palms, papayas and mimosas—and cut the grass with a penknife on his hands and knees, blade by blade. Pedro was badly strapped with six kids, one just born. Another had died of malnutrition the year before and they all had the bulging stomachs and huge hollow eyes of hunger. Pedro had borrowed the equivalent of $2 from Maria some time back, and rather than face the overwhelming task of repaying her, was ready to quit working for us. With his talents he could earn handsomely in a trade, but he let all these possibilities slide out of sight; it was just too hard to think beyond the day, too much to muster the drive and initiative to show up for work regularly as one would have to do, for instance, in a plumbing outfit.

I had met Orlando Leite, the head of the local Conservatory of Music who told me he badly needed cellists for his symphony; there was only one cello player in the entire state. So one morning on my way to market, I dropped by to tell him I'd play with them if they could scare up an instrument (I was a middling cellist). The receptionist leaped up and said "everyone" had been waiting for me. Orlando immediately canceled his piano lesson and rushed me to the lone cellist, Hiram, who, in turn, dismissed his pupil. By then I was definitely leery, but they dragged me in and thrust Hiram's cello into my hands, commanding: "Play!" Actually it wasn't that bad; they called in the first violinist and pianist and we got through a trio that, fortunately, I knew well.

A month later the symphony was scheduled to give a command performance for the rector of the university and other city notables, and suddenly I had to procure a proper white dress. Not so easy; for a frenzied week

I dashed between two dressmakers, having a terrible time between my limited vocabulary and sign language, explaining that I needed a style wide enough so I could wrap my legs around a cello and long enough to be decent (not the current ultra-mini fashion). The first dressmaker was swamped with orders for an upcoming *festa* and could only spare time to cut out the dress, so I had to find a second one willing to sew it. (Their total fee was $1.75.) Then came the almost impossible task of combing stores for the right fabric—with all sorts of adventures along the way, such as our ancient jeep coughing to a halt in rush-hour traffic and my having to hike in the dark to a gas station for a can of petrol. But, after several postponements due to student rioting, the concert finally happened; the orchestra managed, the singers were superb, and the bats swooped back and forth. . . .

Driving a battered Brazilian jeep had also proved fortuitous just at a time when our American confreres in the city (U.S. agronomy consultants), with their conspicuous American cars, were warned, for safety, to stay off the roads during the political upheavals aimed at "exploitative Yankees." On the other hand, Bel (the "villain" responsible for the riots) and I could buzz around incognito.

We had a few glimpses into local institutional procedures. One day Steve was brought home from school with a fractured elbow. During a relay race on the playground he was required to carry on his back a much larger classmate, with disastrous results. For advice we tried to reach the highly recommended pediatrician who ran the children's hospital, but he was out for siesta. So we drove to the hospital and found that *everybody* was out for siesta. After an hour they finally rounded up a radiologist and he spent another hour taking four

X-rays, all excruciating because they had to stretch Steve's arm in different directions. The last straw was when the technician came up from the dark room after the first two to say the photos hadn't come out and he'd have to retake them. Eventually the chief arrived and recommended a bone man who ran another hospital. It took two more hours for him to show up, Steve wailing all the time that he couldn't stand the pain another minute. The orthopedist held off for still another hour, saying he couldn't set the bone right away—had to wait until the swelling stopped. At last they brought Steve into one of the waiting rooms and plopped him on a table, other patients looking on curiously. Though I protested, they insisted that it was necessary to put him to sleep, so this entailed collecting an anesthetist who set up his little portable ether apparatus. Steve breathed dutifully into the mask (reporting afterward that he went off into "another dimension"), and Bel was instructed to hold down his legs, though his own were none too stable at that point. So the cast went on, and two weeks later was off. Despite a good deal of pain, Steve was never severely handicapped; he continued playing soccer and we even wrapped the cast in plastic so he could go part way into the ocean.

These little tales serve to illustrate our days of frantic busyness filled with a million ridiculous, frustrating, but necessary errands. Of course such episodes happen in the U.S., too, but not every day. Here they were the way of life; one was so occupied with coping with the creaky machinery of existence, the process of accomplishing, that if and when the end was reached, often one was too weary to recognize or appreciate it. Or it might just be too late. Thus, if an American set up a clearly defined goal and rushed single-mindedly toward it, he'd fall on his face, die of an ulcer, or take the next plane home.

Brazil was such a land of contrasts. We were constantly aware of the omnipresent juxtaposition of appalling poverty and almost obscene luxury. We were invited to university faculty parties—*lueras* (full moon celebrations) where everyone went a little mad in the balmy air, where the whiskey and coconut "water" flowed, exotic dishes were produced, the red ants bit, and by 4 a.m. most of the guests ended up in the swimming pool, *Dolce Vita* style.

We were encouraged to join one of several social clubs, mainly to take tennis lessons; Eric and Steve got their start there and later went on to become city champions in Milwaukee. But on the way to our Ideal Club, we had to drive past street after street lined with beggars, and walking downtown they pursued us, tugging at our clothes, the women mumbling about a sick husband. Tiny children accompanied their ragged mothers or would go it alone. Others would stand at your elbow even in the more elegant stores and, as you opened your purse to pay for a purchase, would hold out their hands. It was said that women sometimes rented sickly looking kids to attract pity. There were more deformed and crippled cases than I'd seen assembled before: hunchbacks, bowlegs, shrunken limbs, stumps of legs or no legs, the enormous feet of elephantiasis, the crumbled extremities of leprosy. One man I noted for two weeks running had a great open, raw sore swarming with flies; I wondered if he kept scraping it or pouring salt into it so it wouldn't heal. One street was filled exclusively with blind men and women crouched on their haunches selling lottery tickets.

One weekend we were guests of Glaucia, our wealthy landlady, who led a caravan into the desert-like interior to visit her prosperous 11,000-acre plantation where she raised cattle, cotton, fruit trees and sugar cane. We were shown to our traditional sleeping quarters, a whitewashed room furnished only with hooks for the four hammocks we had brought. While the adults lolled on the wide veranda imbibing and nibbling endless varieties of meats and sweets, the kids fished and sailed rafts on a sizable private reservoir, and rode horses and donkeys. Then, on returning to the city, Bel had to face again the tension stirred up by political opponents of his university sponsors over a research project that was branded subversive, where his fearful academic colleagues had begun stashing revolvers in their glove compartments and desks. . . .

Thus, every day during our year in Brazil, we had ample opportunity to observe closeup the dichotomy of have-nots too desiccated to protest, and the affluent idle who chose not to help their own poor, but were expending energy protesting against their brothers north of the border.

My next report will introduce the preoccupation of much of Brazil with "the world beyond the veil," and will detail my own frightening encounter with Macumba (the voodoo of the Northeast), and the necessity of an exorcism.

May 18, 2010

ODYSSEY
Voodoo in Brazil: A Look Behind the Veil of the Spirit World

by Lisa Paulson

Last week I concluded descriptions of the varied adventures of our family of four, living in Northeast Brazil for the year 1967-68. My husband Bel was on a research grant, investigating political practices in the region that would favor economic development. Now I'll introduce the preoccupation of much of Brazil with "the world beyond the veil," detailing my own frightening encounter with macumba, *(the voodoo rites of the Northeast).*

It was Christmas, but it was hard to generate the proper spirit when we had just come in from the heat and sweat of the tennis court. Neighborhood palm trees were bravely festooned with colored lights and a few Portuguese carols wafted across the mimosas from the nearby Baptist church. Our own tree was a jaggy dead branch wrapped in foil and hung with glittery paper ornaments. A fine swim in the ocean and a starlit supper of lobster at a waterfront café completed our holiday agenda.

Then, to approximate something like a Christmas midnight church service, we opted for the exotic: a macumba ceremony. We were invited to attend by Raimunda, leader of the local macumba, who was, coincidentally, also the maid of the Peace Corps doctor in town. We drove to her *favela* or slum area and parked in deep, soft sand. A sky full of stars illuminated white figures flitting in and out of doorways. All was silent except for the muffled thud of our footsteps. We were ushered through a barricade where the white robes were assembling. Raimunda, a petite grandmother, appeared. Suddenly here was no maid but a high priestess in sparkling silver crown, white harem pants, white sneakers and a white satin Batman-type cape embroidered with a shiny blue fish. She was the matriarch of the favela; she made all major decisions, commanded complete allegiance.

We were ushered into the macumba hut and the door was locked (minors were not allowed to watch). Rows of green and white pennants festooned the ceiling, and pictures of the Madonna, Jesus and the saints were pinned over the walls. The tiered altar was jammed with more statues of saints, from St. Francis to St. George on his horse. A number of fish were included (whether this had to do with the early Christian symbol or the marine influence on these people we couldn't figure). Raimunda chalked a star in the center of the dirt floor, then lit dozens of candles on the altar and stuck some around the large "leaning pole" in the middle of the room. The women, in long white satin or embroidered skirts, began to line up on one side, and a few men, also in white, lined the opposite wall. As each woman entered, she lay flat on the floor and kissed the star.

Then the ceremony began, curiously similar to parts of the Roman Catholic Mass. Macumba is a practice that melds the worship of African deities and Catholic saints, along with rituals of the native Indian population. Kneeling, crossing, clapping. Raimunda led the chanting and singing, which began with boys on bongo drums, shakers and triangle at the front. Voices pulsated with responsive Hail Marys, then burst into wild hymns, at times resembling the primitive African chants to which *macumba* is linked. The white figures began to jiggle and twitch in jerky samba-like rhythms. The women rolled and staggered around, falling against others who caught them or kept them from stumbling into lighted candles. Heads went down, faces covered by mops of wild, stringy hair that swept the dirt. An assistant priestess swung a pot of burning incense into everyone's face until the air was so thick we could barely see. Each participant rushed to inhale the smoke and get even dizzier. Raimunda shouted from the altar, inviting each participant to come up to kneel and be blessed and kissed; then they were twirled off, moaning and clinging to the center pole to regain equilibrium. From time to time Raimunda sailed out the door (for liquid fortification?), and finally brought the *cachassa* (rum) bottle back and set it on the altar.

After observing for two hours, Bel and I left, before they got really worked up to the trances where people passed out completely. Apparently they "work" almost the entire night.

The next episode began several months later. Maria, our live-in helper, was sorting beans with me in the kitchen. She asked if I recalled that last Sunday she'd come home and gone straight to her room. She had a terrible headache and lay shivering in her hammock with uncontrollable chills. When she opened her eyes, she saw a tall woman standing close, watching her. Maria thought she might have been dreaming or feverish and fearfully wrapped her hammock tightly around her. But then she felt a tugging, someone plucking at the hammock. Quickly she sat up and saw the woman leaning over her, long black hair streaming down covering her face. Terrified, Maria ran into the kitchen and began pealing carrots, but the crippling pains sent her back to lie down again. Once more the apparition appeared, this time throwing itself on top of Maria, the long hair tangling. Escaping to the kitchen, Maria sat shaking and silent. There were no more visitations, but for several nights the same chill and violent headache would return.

Three days later, Maria's friend Santa stopped by with a young man named Jose. He watched Maria for a while, then said: "You didn't sleep well last Sunday, did you?" No. "You had a bad chill and headache?" Why yes, startled. "There was a woman with long dark hair who appeared in your room, who pulled at your hammock?" Yes, yes! But I never told anyone, not Dona Lisa, not Santa. What does it mean?

Jose, it turned out, was a psychic medium from the local Spiritist center; he knew all, saw all. He told her the apparition was that of her older sister who had died in childbirth, but who wanted to stay close and protect her. Awed, Maria wept. All this she related to me, tears falling into the beans.

Shortly after this, for no apparent reason except maybe a little too much sun, I developed a sudden, intractable illness: a searing headache, tension, burning eyes. I found I was almost entirely paralyzed physically. I had a helpless feeling that I was even losing my mind. Baffled, Bel called in a Brazilian doctor we trusted, but he could find no physical explanation for my symptoms. This went on for a couple of weeks and I began to be terrified that I might not make it out of Brazil alive.

Then one Saturday night, Jose, the Spiritist medium, was visiting in the garden again. Apropos of nothing, he said to Maria: "There's someone sick here with a bad headache, isn't there? Especially bad around the eyes?" Yes. Again, Maria hadn't mentioned this. He concentrated. "She once visited a macumba session, didn't she?" Yes. "And there was some dispute over money with the high priestess?" Maria recalled that I'd borrowed Raimunda's sewing machine in January, and then gave her money the next time I attended a macumba ceremony. Afterward Raimunda said she understood the money was for macumba and that I should have given her more for the sewing. I had felt my offering was ample for both. Anyway, the verdict was that Raimunda—or unconsciously through her "spirit guide"— had put the evil eye on me in that moment of anger. So now there was a departed soul attached to me, someone who had died with a pain in the head, who was inflicting a similar punishment on me, intending to make my life miserable, but not necessarily to do me in. Jose said that because Maria lived with me and was on the way to becoming a medium herself, this spirit was jumping back and forth between us; when I had the headache, she didn't, and vice versa. (We checked this out—correct.) The best way to exorcise the spirit, the medium said, was for me to go to the Spiritist center where he officiated. Since I'd wanted to see this anyway, and they were "working" the following evening, we all decided to go.

Spiritism is a movement created by Frenchman Allan Kardec and imported to Brazil in the late 19th century. It focuses on providing solutions to everyday life problems, both physical and emotional, and on making suffering bearable. Adherents believe there is help from spirits of the dead and from psychic mediums who facilitate this contact. They approach healing holistically and believe in karmic consequences from past behaviors. It is a belief system that appeals to middle and upper classes as rational and scientific, although in Fortaleza, the humble little building we visited had attracted the very poorest in the city.

We piled our boys and Maria and Santa into the jeep and drove out to a favela in the dunes. We found a small mud house, jammed with sweating, tattered humanity on benches in the rear. A bar in front separated the mass of people from the *mesa branca*, a large table covered with a white cloth, around which sat 12 mediums, elbows on the table, hands covering their eyes. We crowded in. Jose spotted us and beckoned me to come sit next to the table; he asked for my exact name. There were few of the gaudy trappings of the macumba in the room. It was bare except for a few standard pictures of Jesus and the Virgin and a large one of St. Joan of Arc. An evangelical-like sermon commenced: exhortations to love your neighbor, live with dignity and honesty even though you were poor and hungry. The congregation was urged to consult with the Spiritist doctors who were daily effecting cures for many afflictions (the Spiritists have their own herbal pharmacies). Next to where I sat was a curtained door with a steady stream of patients ducking through. Sharp groans and wails issued from time to time.

Next began the real business: communicating with departed spirits. Jose and Santa were the chief mediums, intoning overlapping ritual prayers. They moved around the table, touching the head of each medium. This immediately caused the persons seated to tremble violently, their breath coming in rasping pants. They moaned, shrieked and wept, leaping up, clutching their heads. Jose calmed them down and pulled messages from them. Apparently the spirits were "coming down" and entering one or another of the mediums, speaking in voices turned gravelly and alien. Jose, catching a message, called out: "Who is there here called Marina? There is a spirit who wants to talk to Marina!"

A final bell sounded and the entire assembly, eyes closed, heads raised, broke out in a long, earnest hymn. Someone turned up the wick on the kerosene lantern swinging overhead, and the mediums were instructed at last to lay their hands down on the table palms up (a few had to be assisted back to reality). I wasn't at all sure whether my "case" had been pleaded. On the way home, I asked Maria if she knew what had happened. She said, "Didn't you see those people going into the curtained-off room? That's where the really bad spirits were dealt with by the Spiritist doctors. Your spirit was treated there."

And, amazingly, as we drove back to the city, I noticed that my paralysis was gradually disappearing and the headache was gone. I have no idea what did the trick—whether the exorcism worked, or it was power of suggestion, or simply coincidence. The important thing was that, thankfully, I was cured.

All this was anthropologically interesting, and, in retrospect, even humorous, but definitely not so at the time! When Bel returned to the local, American-educated medical doctor to recite what had happened, he was told that this was a common occurrence, that such situations could not be explained by modern medicine.

For much of my life, I'd had intimations of a mysterious dimension existing below the radar of our own largely scientific society. Sometimes this surfaced as conventional faith, but there was the occasional dip into quirky mysticism. In Northeast Brazil, where three cultures have come together—Portuguese and African descendents, along with the indigenous Indians—there is a conviction that the veil separating this world from the next is very thin. I definitely sensed that because this belief was so prevalent, the spirit world was indeed closer there than at home, and most people, including the more educated and sophisticated, performed superstitious little rituals "just in case" (like placing lighted candles on the sidewalk).

As soon as I was back in the U.S., I felt that multi-dimensional, colorful openness receding in the face of our cool, skeptical society. Perhaps this is our loss.

Findhorn's nature sanctuary for meditation and Taizé a capella singing

May 25, 2010

ODYSSEY
A Great Hunger for the Findhorn Story

by Lisa Paulson

Last week I left you with the tale of my unsettling encounter with "otherworldly" dimensions through Brazilian voodoo (macumba) and the imported French movement called Spiritism, offering solutions to everyday problems through the intervention of departed spirits and mediums.

After a year in Brazil, our family returned to Milwaukee in the summer of 1968. While Bel plunged back into running his Urban Community Development department at UWM and teaching political science on campus, we also soon discovered an intriguing new school in the city. Called Psy-Bionics, it was teaching altered states of consciousness.

We thought this might be a way to continue our exploration of the transpersonal areas that had opened to us when I was seemingly caught in an evil eye spell and had to be exorcised in Northeast Brazil.

Bel and I and our two boys all took this course in mental imaging, and the results for each one of us were so compelling that I jumped in to work with the instructor to develop the school. We had found that at a subconscious level one could apparently direct outcomes for health and other life conditions by imagining specific goals while in a deeply relaxed state—and believing them possible. We also saw how these techniques might be accessing some of those

Belden and Lisa Paulson   81

supernatural areas I'd experienced in Brazil. Among the mushrooming activities of Psy-Bionics, we sponsored a number of large conferences that brought in noted psychologists and investigators in paranormal research from around the country. Interestingly, over and over we heard them talking about an unusual place in Scotland called Findhorn. This was a community of some 300 people engaged in what these scientists were calling "one of the most important spiritual experiments in the world."

I listened, fascinated by wild stories of how oversized and unusual plants were being grown in beach sand not far from the Arctic Circle. What made this possible was the step-by-step instruction received in meditation by the founders of this group. In 1962 a middle-aged British couple and their Canadian friend were instructed to bring their ancient trailer to the dunes near the fishing village of Findhorn and plant a garden. It seemed that direct communication was established with the patterning life force in each species of plant. The response had been so amazing that, as word got out, people from all over the world had converged on this desolate corner of northeast Scotland to find out for themselves what this "Factor X" might be and to practice living in this kind of conscious cooperation with nature.

Quickly I boned up on Findhorn, read the few published books, and realized that I simply had to go there—by myself. It was an essential next step for me. It was a quest to clarify the next steps of my life.

In the fall of 1976, I flew off to Scotland. Beyond all the stories of mystical happenings, what I actually experienced far exceeded my expectations. Quickly I was made aware of the purpose of the community: "to redress the balance between people and nature,"

recognizing the intrinsic interrelationship and interdependence of all the elements of life on earth. More was going on than simply growing unusual plants. In the three weeks I lived and worked in the community, I began to see in clearer perspective my old personal habits and constructs, and for the first time could actually step away from them. Letting go of my usual chewing over baggage from the past and anxiously planning for the future, I experienced the feeling of stepping into a river of energy and "knowing," and letting myself be swept along in that present moment—trusting that whatever the outcome, it would be the right one. This was a switch from fixing goals, as we had practiced at Psy-Bionics; I began to see that perhaps there were intelligences at work that knew better than I what needed to happen, better than I might "program" on my own.

Settling in among the jumble of bungalows and aging trailers that made up the Findhorn community, I found that people have been coming here from every belief— or non-belief—system. They're drawn to this place of palpable power and energy in order to follow the practice of being constantly mindful of living in harmony with all they touch, bringing gentleness and caring to every task and interaction.

How all these diverse paths converge is through community members being together in silence—each person listening to his/her own quiet, inner voice that connects to a wisdom or intelligence transcending individual beliefs, sidestepping personal baggage or bias that might get in the way of coming to clear answers that are in the highest interest of everyone. A bit like a Quaker meeting, it's how they make group decisions: intuitively, rather than voting from a conscious, mental level.

In the early 1970s, the emphasis at Findhorn shifted from the glamorous myths about big vegetables to "growing people with a new consciousness." An extensive array of educational offerings have been organized over the years, so now there is a continuous stream of visitors coming for shorter or longer stays to investigate any number of topics, some programs in foreign languages. Thousands of people now have the chance to experience a different and eminently graceful way of life. The basic program, which I went through, is called "Experience Week"—where participants can hear members talk about the philosophy and ideas and initiatives, and then can put these into practice immediately by pitching into the daily life of the community.

It was on that initial Findhorn visit in 1976 that I first began to hear serious discussions about the impending global environmental crises such as global warming and dwindling fossil fuels. At a week-long international conference I attended that brought 300 outside participants (titled "World Crisis and the Wholeness of Life"), renowned presenters spoke of how we were foolishly living off our "principal" (non-renewable resources) when we should be living on the "interest"—renewables like the sun and wind. We heard about "sustainability" when it was still an esoteric jargon term, long before it was a concept widely accepted and applied. In recent years this deep respect for nature has translated into projects that have addressed sustainability issues not only within the community itself, but also have looked at problems worldwide.

Today, Findhorn's state-of-the-art ecological village is perhaps the strongest and purest model in Britain, reportedly, with the smallest carbon footprint. The community supplies its own energy with two giant Vesta wind generators and photovoltaic panels, and recycles its sewage with a "living machine"—a biological waste treatment system in a greenhouse that runs material through a series of tanks with fish, plants and bacteria, producing almost drinkable water at the end.

The idea of living with integrity and honesty in relationships with others, and seeing sacredness and beauty in the ordinary, means approaching both grand and menial jobs with equal enthusiasm, and caring meticulously for the materials and tools one works with. Any line between work and play vanishes, because everything one does is seen as important and exhilarating. This is what I experienced during the three weeks I was there, letting go of old patterns and opening up to entirely new modes of thinking and being. I spent days happily digging a ditch in freezing sleet and rain, lovingly brushing and oiling my tools before I hung them up in the shed. Then I worked in the kitchen where I took utensils from drawers labeled "wooden beings" and "metal beings," and I mixed dough in a huge machine named "Hobart." There was recognition that everything contains natural material that on some level has a kind of consciousness—that can be reached and communicated with. The attitude with which one approaches a task is critical. I heard the story of how the giant Gestetner copier in the publishing building shut down cold every time a certain guest walked past. One day we were eating lunch outside and I was about to set my bowl of steaming hot soup on the lawn when a member reprimanded me: "Not on the grass!" You know how some people are in tune with their cars, or how some have a "black thumb" when it comes to making plants grow? Well, you get the idea. . . . Findhorn folks understand this, pay attention, and nourish their relationship to all they touch.

At the end of my three weeks at Findhorn, I was still in awe of the palpable energy I felt, the sense of well-being everyone seemed to exude. They positively glowed, and it was catching. I'd met or was exposed to all the legendary figures I'd heard about. At the conference I attended I'd listened to sophisticated analyses of the challenges facing all of us, individually and collectively. I'd heard about intelligent solutions that were light years beyond where the mainstream stood. I saw how important it would be in the future to learn to conserve and recycle; to share tasks such as the growing and preparing of food; to pool tools and equipment; to live with common walls and land and wells—as one can do in an "intentional" community such as Findhorn (defined as a group of people who come together with a shared vision and purpose and a commitment to live these values together).

My last day in Scotland found me struggling against a gale-force wind and driving rain to the top of a sand dune overlooking the roiling North Sea below. I was wrestling with the knowledge that I couldn't go back to the United States to the same life I'd left just three weeks before. Working and interacting with people from every part of the globe, people who clearly were living in close and constant attunement to nature, had turned my life upside down and, at age 48, had changed me irrevocably. All I could do was stand there with rain streaming down my face and shout into the gale: "Okay, I give up. I know I have to take these radical ideas I've been exposed to home to Wisconsin. I know this is what I'm meant to do with my life. But I'll need help, because, hey, I haven't a clue how to begin!"

And, as when something is right, I was shown, step-by-step. It turned out that back home there was a great hunger for the story of Findhorn, and I was drafted to give many slide talks around our region.

Shortly after I returned, I experienced another of the many uncanny examples of synchronicity that had surprised me constantly in Scotland. The phone rang and a voice said, "This is Angelynn Brown. Do you remember that we met at Findhorn? I had a dream last week that I was to leave the community immediately and move to Milwaukee to do spiritual work with you." (I recalled that when I heard there was a Findhorn member from my hometown, Milwaukee, I had looked her up; she was busily running the community kitchen, and we chatted just briefly.)

Soon after the call, Angelynn showed up on our doorstep and lived with us for the next several years. She played a pivotal role in helping me to interpret Findhorn and its philosophy. Together we organized study groups and gave talks around the area. She was instrumental in helping to publicize a major event bringing the founders of the community to Milwaukee, an event that would indeed usher in a new chapter in my life and for many, many others.

Our flagship bioshelter attracts visitors

June 1, 2010

ODYSSEY
The Idea for High Wind Is Born—
A Partnership with the University

by Belden Paulson

B.J. Lisa obviously had a profound experience during her three weeks at Findhorn, the "New Age" community in Scotland, in fall 1976. She had been dubious about some of the tales she'd heard and wanted to check these out for herself. Already she'd had a traumatic encounter in Northeast Brazil with a voodoo-type experience known as *macumba* and had helped to found Psy-Bionics, a school in Milwaukee teaching altered states of consciousness. On returning from Findhorn she felt that she was a different person.

Q. How did you take to all of this? Did you feel that maybe you had "lost" your wife after Findhorn? Could this have an impact on your position at the university? What were the long-run implications for your life together and your work?

A. I was very perplexed. We'd been married for more than 20 years, but I'd never seen her so fired up. I wasn't even sure about the best questions to ask that would explain the Findhorn experience.

In those days, the latter 1970s, the New Age had not yet become an over-used cliché.

I'd read enough, all confirmed by her scraps of notes, that the New Age means recognizing that mutual cooperation and respect among all living systems is essential if our planet is to survive. Our intellect and greed and selfishness and lust for power have gotten in the way of a more inclusive awareness. Lisa quoted David Spangler, one of the speakers at the Findhorn conference, who had written in his book, *Revelation: The Birth of a New Age*: "The New Age is fundamentally a change of consciousness from one of isolation and separation to one of communion, attunement, wholeness." All of this made sense to me.

Obviously, Lisa feared she might soon be dragged back from the heights of such powerful idealism into the mainstream culture of compromise and competition. At this time, I myself was at a point of some openness to alternative thinking. I had joined the University of Wisconsin in the early 1960s and was heavily involved now in dealing with inner-city poverty and racism. I had begun to question whether the university, and the mainstream culture generally, had the capacity to respond to today's intractable problems without a radical shift in thinking.

Several months after Lisa's return from Scotland, she talked me into driving to Chicago to attend a lecture by Peter Caddy, the former RAF officer who was a co-founder of Findhorn. I was impressed by Peter's down-to-earth talk about the community's successes and challenges and his idealism about serving the planet with a new sense of compassion and interconnectedness. A short time later, I happened to meet with a professor in the university's school of engineering who had just received a grant to explore advanced thinking on the interrelationship between technology and culture. I introduced him to the Findhorn story with its emphasis on

radical lifestyle changes. I mentioned E.F. Schumacher, another of the Findhorn speakers, whose seminal book, *Small Is Beautiful*, advocated "appropriate technology"—technology relevant to the situation at hand—which also implied frugality and encouraged self-sufficiency. The professor was intrigued and asked me to represent the university on a planning committee for a major conference coming up in Chicago, to be keynoted by Schumacher in spring 1977.

Some 2,300 people came to hear Schumacher and to participate in 60 other lectures and workshops about appropriate technology. We'd reserved a room for maybe 15 people where Lisa could report on Findhorn; to our astonishment, 400 folks lined the corridor demanding a larger space. Next to Schumacher, Lisa's Findhorn presentation was the big event of the conference. I had invited one of my deans, who was so enthusiastic about her workshop that he urged me to organize educational programs around these ideas at the university.

Since people in Wisconsin were thirsty for information, in June 1977 we got the university to sponsor talks by Peter Caddy and his co-founder wife, Eileen. In the largest available space on campus, they wowed the 1,200 attendees—students and faculty as well as people from business, government and civic organizations. In short order I got approvals from university officials to begin lining up a series of seminars, not only for traditional students but also for the larger community. To teach with me, we invited David Spangler—philosopher and author—and his Yugoslav colleague, artist/musician Milenko Matanovic (who had left Findhorn and were in the U.S. heading the new Lorian Association). They soon moved to Milwaukee with their families. Two of our early courses were breakthroughs on subjects entirely new to our conventional academic curricula: Planetary Survival and the Role of Alternative Communities, and New Dimensions of Governance—Images of Holistic Community. At a time when campus classes were losing enrollments, these were dramatically oversubscribed.

As increasing numbers flocked to the many courses and workshops in Milwaukee we dreamed up, we began hearing the comment: "We're seminared out. We've had enough sitting around talking in classrooms. Time is running out for the environment. We need to do something *practical!*"

That's when we established the nonprofit High Wind Association whose function was to demonstrate the practicality of renewable energy, to work with the land as an integral ecosystem, to live simply and frugally, and—at the same time—to cosponsor educational programs on these issues with the university. It was then that Lisa and I decided to make available for this purpose our rundown 46-acre farm southwest of Plymouth.

In the summer of 1977, with two friends, we visited the projects of the New Alchemy Institute on Cape Cod and Prince Edward Island in Canada. We wanted to see their two experimental "bioshelters," state-of-the-art passive solar buildings that contained a residence as well as an attached production greenhouse. New Alchemy was a pioneering group focusing on renewable energy, energy-efficient construction, and sustainable agriculture. The bioshelter was designed to *produce,* rather than consume, energy. Scientists there convinced us to try something comparable in Wisconsin.

By the end of 1978 I was realizing, like Lisa, that I was no longer the same person I'd been. When Lisa decided on a return visit to Findhorn, I went along and participated in a weeklong intensive living experience in the community. My contact with the leaders and residents convinced me of the significance of this kind of model for rethinking the future of our culture, indeed of the world. My intimate collaboration with David and Milenko and many others deepened my perceptions of reality far beyond anything I had learned at Oberlin College and the University of Chicago.

From many folks I had heard about Spangler's mystical proclivities and had read his books, including this passage in his influential early publication, *Revelation,* which helped to conceptualize the meaning of the New Age:

> *For most of my early life I have been conscious of two worlds, two aspects of reality. One is the so-called normal world, revealed to us through our five senses and their technological extensions. The other is a super-sensory reality, a metaphysical world of light and energy and essence, home to intelligences more evolved than our own in many cases. This might be called a spiritual or even a mystical dimension, entered through intuition and meditation . . . a world behind the world known to our physical senses.*

While as a fairly hardheaded social scientist I could readily comprehend all of the dimensions of Findhorn in terms of its social organization and governance, and, of course, its educational programs, I still had to overcome my skepticism about this "other dimension" that Spangler brought. Yet I felt this was the key to the magnetism that drew people to Findhorn and now was drawing people to our "new work" (however vaguely defined). I felt this deeper reality had some relation to Lisa's traumatic experience with *macumba* in Brazil that could not be explained by the medical doctor, and the remarkable results people experienced using altered states of consciousness at Psy-Bionics. As I got closer to David and his colleagues and began to understand his esoteric world, I felt that my personal transformation was being informed by the centrality of this consciousness or Spirit. Later, when I wrote my memoir, *Odyssey*, the underlying theme throughout the book is that economic and political strategies are essential, but it's the "X Factor" of consciousness that is the critical determinant.

With a shift in my personal priorities and understanding of the urgency of some major societal changes, we decided to bring the New Alchemy architect to Plymouth to give us ideas for our own possible bioshelter. He flew out and assisted in drawing up a grant proposal that we then submitted to the appropriate technology program of the U.S. Department of Energy. In 1980 we were awarded a small grant of $25,000.

When we convened a meeting on a blustery evening in February 1981 in Milwaukee to announce the grant and to seek volunteers, over a hundred people showed up. Immediately, an experienced carpenter agreed to be lead builder for the bioshelter construction, and a teacher/gardener came to grow food to support the workers. Soon a Ph.D. psychologist signed on to help manage the household operation, including the kitchen. Suddenly the farm was humming with activity. Our old turn-of-the-century farmhouse had become what we called the "pressure cooker," with ten residents and two dogs, soon spilling out into the big barn and renovated chicken coop. What started as an ad hoc construction gang soon evolved into

what we came to realize was an "intentional community." Since we had used our grant for building materials, all those who came to work with us had to be volunteers.

Whenever I went to a university meeting, I was asked about High Wind. There was curiosity, even fascination, about the intention of starting a holistic community (whatever that meant). People were impressed that the U.S. government had invested in this solar building, and that we'd become a magnet for hordes of volunteers who even quit their jobs to get involved. Then there was the fact that UWM's recently retired chancellor was helping us with fund-raising. Above all, they couldn't fathom how our classes were drawing huge numbers when campus enrollments were declining.

Since my dean was supportive of my department's work, he wanted to know more about the new kinds of learning we were promoting. I had to convince the university attorney that there was no personal conflict of interest, even though some seminars took place at High Wind, in the town of Mitchell, on property owned by Lisa and me. Because we played major roles in High Wind's unfolding growth, I had to submit documents proving that there was no personal financial gain. Instead, we were helping to finance this evolving enterprise. While I continued working full-time at the university, Lisa's commitment as a volunteer at High Wind was full-time. With our other volunteers, we all functioned as a team.

The university had only begun to understand my growing interest in Futures Studies, and none of us had yet fully comprehended the challenges of creating and living in an intentional community.

Community meeting in the big experimental dome—the "igloo."

JUNE 15, 2010

ODYSSEY
Intentional Community Requires Intense Effort

by Belden Paulson

B.J. With the lofty vision brought back from Findhorn by your wife Lisa, and establishment of the nonprofit High Wind Association, and award of a Department of Energy grant to build a novel solar structure, some volunteers from Milwaukee arrived at your land outside Plymouth as a construction gang and with interest in the concept of "intentional community"—where a group coalesces with a shared vision and purpose and a commitment to live out this purpose.

Q. What happened next? Starting from scratch, you must have encountered a bunch of problems. With a very heterogeneous group of presumably idealistic volunteers, some of *whom you barely knew, how did you all get along? What were your own biggest personal challenges as the project evolved?*

A. First, I'll talk about some of the issues that came up for me, and later in the article I'll ask Lisa to come in to describe some of our other early challenges, including a searing incident that threatened to tear our embryonic community apart.

As our initial construction group gradually evolved into an intentional community, with a number of the volunteers not returning to their old jobs, a host of sticky community issues began to surface. Sometimes they ended up focusing on Lisa and me. After all, we had started the whole enterprise, we owned the property, even though High Wind had full use of all the initial 46 acres, and some of it we had donated to the nonprofit. When serious financial bottlenecks occurred, we usually stepped in to help. Often it came down to an issue of perception: Who really held the power?

This challenge became crystal clear when Lisa and I had occasion to revisit Findhorn, where we participated in a panel for founders of six well-known communities around the world. The panel articulated a universal issue all the founders faced—the so-called "Founders Syndrome." This was the tension between the originators who had articulated the vision and purpose, and community members who rightly wanted to make the experience their own. This might mean seeking to reframe community goals and challenging the initial leadership.

High Wind, like all the communities on the panel, emphasized its commitment to non-hierarchical leadership and governance by consensus. I can't recall a single High Wind community decision reached by consensus that Lisa and I overturned, even if we could have. But there were many intense debates during the often-interminable meetings to reach consensus. On several occasions when we felt the community might be falling apart, with factions developing, and we were unsure of our own proper role, we sought counsel from experienced friends, including some from Findhorn. Their response was always the same: Founders hold responsibility to sound a clear note about the vision. If there are members with other visions, they should be respected but invited to leave and create their own groups.

Another big personal issue became ever clearer as residents at the farm evolved from the original crew of builders into an intentional community. Some people were production/goal oriented, while others were more concerned with the process of getting there. Obviously, both were essential, but at times one or the other approach took over and, in my view, sometimes became extreme. For example, sometimes Lisa leaned toward the process mode, which meant slowing down and taking care of the ever-present human dimensions. Often I was so concerned about all the challenges in front of us, and the fact that I held a lot of responsibility for "results," that I could go too far in the direction of just "getting it done." Some of us became impatient when evening sessions were convened where we were all required to "share our pain," even if at the time we (I) didn't feel any pain or didn't want to share it. I could be labeled as someone with "thick skin," insensitive to those with "thin skins" who were easily hurt by life's experiences and by negative responses from others.

I welcomed our periodic "internal conferences," sometimes with an outside resource person, where each of us could freely express his/her needs and wishes and gripes. Lisa and I, as much or more than other community members, got a healthy dose of criticism. She might be pilloried for her lofty visions, expressed through editorials in our community newsletter, *Windwatch,* that aimed to lift the spirits of the residents out of their daily grind and to remind us all of our initial values and goals. I received even more censure, in part because I was often introducing ideas and plans for ambitious educational programs or other initiatives that scared the community, and which they thought too hard to carry out. Also, when someone else came up with a project and I said, "Great idea, you do it," this was often interpreted as code for "I don't think it will work and I don't want to get involved." So they would drop the idea.

The most significant issue I had to confront as the years passed was the realization that I was not too adept at intentional community group dynamics. While visionary thinking was what High Wind was all about, this could be intimidating and, among some residents, even oppressive. All agreed that while the community's mission was imperative, the process of getting there was at least as important as the results and we needed to be careful to find a balance. The qualities that were optimally required for my approach didn't always fit too well into the conventional dynamics of an intentional community.

Notwithstanding the challenges, the High Wind community was an extraordinarily exciting place. Dedicated folks were converging at the farm to give their all. Our passive solar bioshelter was moving toward realization as a usable space and an important environmental demonstration of a building that produces energy. For a while the media had made High Wind its darling. Residents were very aware of the various dysfunctionalities of modern life and were seeking a new way to see and be in the world. For me this endeavor merited my full energy, but I couldn't give it my total attention because I also held a full-time university job. We all recognized that High Wind was one place where a person could come to *take a stand*. What we were attempting to create had more potential than anything else I was aware of, while acknowledging that there was a huge gap between the vision and the reality on the ground.

In the next column Lisa will address the delicate subjects of personal sustenance and gender issues as they came up at High Wind, describing in particular one incident that shook us all up.

Marcia facilitates the Game of Life to help us decide future directions

June 17, 2010

ODYSSEY
People, Issues, and Relationships at High Wind

by Lisa Paulson

B.J. In 1976 you brought a vision back from Findhorn that, with the help of many enthusiastic volunteers, led to the establishment of the rural High Wind community near Plymouth.

Q. What were some of the issues that came up with a group of idealistic volunteers living and working very intensely in close quarters, and how did you all deal with them?

A. At first, everybody in the community did everything together. We got to wear many hats and learned multiple skills—as builders, gardeners, cooks, group and event facilitators, communicators. Gradually, though, members began to specialize and, as the years piled up, besides the educational programs that involved us all, various private businesses were created, both at High Wind and in Milwaukee.

Those volunteers living at High Wind found various ways to stay afloat. Some had saved a small nest egg. Others found part-time jobs in the area. There were couples where one partner worked outside the community while the other could be a full-time volunteer. For example, because Bel taught at the university, I could devote all my time to being the outreach person and could garden, run tours and edit our journal, *Windwatch,* which chronicled what we were doing and thinking.

Then there were some residents who thought if we were here to demonstrate simple living, it made little sense to commute away from the land, and they looked for ways to earn a livelihood on-site. Don Austin, a retired school principal from Chicago, had always wanted to work with his hands, so he created a shop in one of our barns and built futons, eventually opening a store in Milwaukee to sell his woodcraft. A young couple, Peter and Bernadette Seely, arrived with their small baby, with the hope of pursuing organic agriculture. Eventually they started what we believe was one of the first CSA (Community Supported Agriculture) programs in the Midwest, selling produce directly to individuals on a subscription-delivery basis. The subscribers to the Seelys' (now privately owned and operated) Springdale Farm presently number over 650. They become involved in supporting the farmers who grow their food, often coming out to help plant and harvest. Jan Masaros came to High Wind in the late 1980s with sophisticated computer knowledge and set up a desktop publishing business with David Lagerman's wife, Louise Mann. Marcia Kjos created a weaving studio and shop to sell crafts and books in the basement of the bioshelter. A few of our folks worked part time at High Wind Books & Records, a store established in Milwaukee in 1984, both to showcase our work and to make alternative ideas, books and materials available in the city. From the very beginning, David Lagerman took on the role of technical coordinator, cutting in half his hours as research librarian at *The Milwaukee Journal* to spend more time at the site.

Besides those mentioned above, the long roster of full-time volunteer residents—couples, singles, kids—added immensely to the richness of the community over the years. You'd find them digging in the gardens, splitting wood, tending farm animals, struggling with paperwork, anchoring our spiritual and celebratory life, becoming pivotal "go-to" resources, mediating disputes, carpentering/ renovating the buildings, holding the kitchen together, meeting visitors, leading tours, and always sprucing up and beautifying forgotten corners.

Roles in the community were not sexist; there were very competent women farmers and men who enjoyed cooking. There was no pressure for guys to be "manly." In fact, we women were happy to see the men become more vulnerable, showing feelings, being demonstrative. In our first year, however, an incident of the men asserting raw power over women shook everyone and taught us to be extra vigilant lest this happen again.

The episode involved certain design elements of the bioshelter mandated by Lillian Leenhouts, our volunteer architect, a nationally known solar expert. One of these was the use of concrete decking for the greenhouse loft space to provide thermal mass, as well as being more durable and moisture resistant than wood. Jim Priest, our very able lead builder, and other men in charge of construction chose to ignore this directive. They brushed aside Betsy Abert and me who were protesting vigorously, and proceeded on their own to build the loft of wood. They said the donation of the Spancrete, which I'd negotiated, was just too late and they had already started nailing the trusses for the greenhouse floor. Cold weather was approaching, they noted, and the building had to be closed in fast. They claimed it wasn't a question of gender, but to us women, this certainly seemed to be a factor.

There were many meetings. It came down to which one—Jim or Lillian—both furious, would pull out, and ultimately we knew we couldn't afford to lose Jim. At that point, and also over a critical change in the roof design without her knowledge, our architect stepped away from the project.

This incident really unnerved everyone and prompted us to look squarely at our interpersonal relationships. We committed to work seriously on negative feelings and held special sessions just for processing them. We tried to be careful about criticizing each other, although reflecting both honestly and lovingly what we saw was part of the openness we sought. With the help of outside mediators who led us in eye-opening "active listening" exercises, and other often painful confrontations and admissions, we forced ourselves to take risks and found we couldn't hide our quirks, we couldn't play face-saving games or indulge in power plays.

The result was that consciousness was definitely raised a few notches, and I believe we shaped up in the personal growth department. We set out to transform negativity with caring and transparency and to understand better the synergy principle that the whole is greater than the sum of its parts. All this, of course, was the ideal and not easily accomplished, but it was the goal to which we were committed.

ODYSSEY
New Breed of Politicians Needed

by Belden Paulson

Q. You are sharing descriptions of how diffi-cult it is to involve others in what seem to be practical visions. And you don't seem afraid to tell how doing so has opened you to confron-tations and personal pain.

This is also a common problem for every-body in local government. As a professional political educator, with the practical High Wind experience near Plymouth in your hip pocket, what would you say to people who want to run for town, village, city, county or school board election?

A. The obvious first response to your challenging question: Why did the per-son decide to run in the first place, be it in a local election, or for higher office? I think the motivations, the real goals, are crucial. I've written previously about how our High Wind experiment evolved, and now I want to use our thinking and way of life as a possible example of what a truly dedicated political aspirant might want to take a look at.

While the little band of volunteers who left their jobs to come to the land near Plymouth 30 years ago to form an inten-tional community had diverse reasons, one fundamental motive was this: They were try-ing to create or model a new vision of soci-ety. They were ordinary people dedicated to

an extraordinary goal. They might not have articulated it quite this way, but there was the idea of sharing resources in contrast to grabbing all they could get for themselves. There was a willingness to listen to people whose ideas they might not accept but with whom, nevertheless, they would cooperate. They participated in making decisions based on reaching consensus (no small undertak-ing) rather than using majority-minority voting where, in effect, one side loses. There was also a strong dedication to preserving the earth and conserving the bounty of nature—not just talking about it, but com-mitting to a simplified and sustainable indi-vidual and collective lifestyle.

I guess many or most folks who enter politics and run for office may begin with somewhat similar goals. They are commit-ted to social justice rather than a win-lose dynamic, to enlightened human relation-ships and governance rather than to political gridlock. They intend to act to preserve the environment rather than succumb to paral-ysis about climate change and energy poli-cy. They want to use their talents to build a better neighborhood and world. Neverthe-less, beyond the rhetoric the big question is: How willing are they, really, to go out on a limb to run as a new kind of elected leader? After all is said and done, will they fall into the ways of the old political system, which, more and more, honest observers think has become dysfunctional? Or do they really want to try to make a difference, whatever it takes? Are they going to become just one more elected official, or will they commit fully to something more—maybe something radical?

Elected leaders are coming out of a culture they may not agree with, but unless they're prepared to work hard to build a new constituency, they'll probably go along with it in order to stay in the race and be re-elected. They face overwhelming pressure to fit into the mainstream culture, which is reinforced by the mass media. The new political leaders would have to challenge the voters to make their innovative agendas work—an uphill battle. A friend of mine who used to represent East Side Milwaukee in Congress regularly told me that he'd love to sponsor legislation embracing our High Wind values, but said there was no constituency; "You'd lose your congressman in the next election."

Now I'd like to return to your original question regarding someone's decision to run for elective office. I'll use a rather dramatic example that happens to relate not to a local election but to running for president of the United States. I mention this because I had a small personal input, and it does have relevance for local politics. (This vignette is detailed in my book, *Odyssey of a Practical Visionary*.)

In March 1980 I received a late-night call from a prominent leader in California who had recently talked to Governor Jerry Brown. Brown was campaigning for president, but if he didn't win the primary in Wisconsin, it was all over. Some people labeled Brown a "flake" or "Governor Moonbeam"—somebody not to be taken seriously. This leader, a member of the university Board of Regents in California and a world-class futurist thinker, told me that the critics could be wrong; Brown had a lot to offer. He asked me to convene informally a microcosm of the leadership in southeast Wisconsin—politicians of every stripe, church folks, academics, the press, business people—to meet Brown and hear him out. He represented views not evident elsewhere, and I was told they were in harmony with those of High Wind.

Brown arrived in Milwaukee on March 7 with an entourage of 15 workers and a security detail. The others left and he settled in at our house where he stayed for two nights. That evening he leaned on the mantel in front of our fireplace for more than three hours, mostly expounding but also dialoguing with the some 50 people gathered. After the formal meeting, he chatted until 11 p.m. and then continued on with a few of us until the small hours. It was a tour de force.

A *Milwaukee Journal* reporter covered the meeting and wrote a long piece. Here's a sample he quoted from Brown:

> *The old system, old assumptions, old values no longer apply . . . It is a threatening idea to those who identify with the old system . . . [which is] planned obsolescence, waste and pollution. We need to be more frugal, more self-reliant, more caring about others . . . We need a new path to stop the competitive web, environmental exhaustion, international hatred. . . . The power of change lies not with the government but with individuals transforming themselves and their government. . . .*

Before folks finally left, including some of the usual skeptics, I asked for feedback.

The general comment: "If someone like Brown were elected, American politics would change almost overnight."

The next day I followed him around to various campaign stops—labor unions, hospitals, a factory. I should not have been shocked, but I was. At each stop he told that particular interest group exactly what they wanted to hear, with the same rhetoric as the other politicians. The previous night's discussion was history, apparently good for our select audience but not for the "real" world.

When he returned to our house the second night, we talked for a couple of hours. I gave him a rundown of Wisconsin's political history. Because I knew I'd never have another chance and we were unwinding after a long day, and he asked for my observations, I decided to share what I really felt:

Jerry, you have the opportunity to take a stand as a new kind of politician. I heard this from many folks who met you here last night. You can't imagine the impact you could have. You're still young, you're dynamic, politically savvy, well-known, and from a respected political family (his father Pat had been a popular governor in California). But your talks today were the same old stuff. You blew it. There was nothing to differentiate you from every other political candidate. Was our meeting last night just "BS" on your part? We thought it came from your heart.

He responded:

To be candid, I didn't come to Wisconsin to be a new kind of politician. I came to lay the groundwork for winning the primary and to save my campaign. I have a lot of volunteers who came from around the country to help me win. They have no money; they're sleeping at the Y

or wherever. Some may be interested in what you say, but I regret to say that this is the way politics works.

I told him he had little chance to win the Wisconsin primary, but he could represent a new breed in the Democratic Party. He shrugged, as if to say, "Your analysis makes sense, but you're asking me to live in a world that doesn't exist."

He won 12 percent of the Wisconsin primary in April, and then withdrew his candidacy.

Just before the November election, Brown returned to Wisconsin to give a tepid endorsement of Jimmy Carter, the Democratic nominee. We met for a few minutes at a downtown hotel. I asked if he remembered our late-night conversation. He said, "You were right. That's what I should have done, but at the time it seemed impossible."

That was 30 years ago. Since then, he has held various offices in local and state government, and now is the Democratic candidate for governor of California in the election next November.

Many of us were convinced that Jerry Brown wanted to become a new kind of political leader, as he eloquently portrayed himself that night at our house. But as he admitted, he was locked into operating like his peers in the prevailing political system. He was not yet ready to take on the hard work of educating and creating a new supportive constituency that could elect him. We'll see what happens next fall.

It seemed to us that there were many thirsty people out there to give him a hand. This could be the case for any courageous, aspiring person who is motivated to run for office as a maverick with an entirely different set of values. Unhappily, many politicians are usually the *last* ones to lead with innovative ideas. Because societal change takes heavy lifting, it's quite possible, although not inevitable, that this new kind of candidate might lose.

My answer, then, to an idealistic politician: America badly needs you to run for office, on any level—not as an ordinary politician but to take up the challenge to build a better world! The central question remains: *Be clear as to why you want to run.*

ODYSSEY
The Idea of an Alternative Think Tank

by Belden Paulson

B.J. In your last column you discussed the need for a new breed of politician. In your book you also explore the need for a new kind of think tank. This emerged from your participation in various University of Wisconsin entities examining roles in higher education.

Q. How did these initial university experiences end up with your working on the far-out idea of organizing a national conference in New York to create a "New Synthesis Think Tank?"

A. The think tank enterprise generated a level of interest way beyond anything we bargained for. But let me start at the beginning.

As a university faculty member who taught seminars on futurist thinking, over the years I was selected to serve on several commissions organized by chancellors and deans on the future of higher education. These included, "The Wisconsin Idea in the 21st Century," the "President's Telecommunications Task Force," and the high-powered "Committee on the Future Directions for the UW-Madison Campus." The most impressive effort, organized by the chancellor of UW-Extension, was to plan a futures conference to draw in 150 university and civic leaders statewide, "to be in the forefront

of examining the relevant emerging issues—economic, social, environmental and cultural—and to determine their impact on the people of Wisconsin, the nation and the world." For this ambitious goal, I participated over months in a small planning group to structure the two-day meeting that would cover an immense range of issues.

As I thought about these varied commissions, I recognized that they all used a kind of "think tank" approach. They would involve teams in task-force settings to go beyond mere superficial discussion and digestion of information at hand to marshal and apply expertise to confront real problems of public importance. With today's complexity of problems, the high stakes of failure, and the seeming public powerlessness to find solutions, there was increasing pressure to push decision-makers to employ think tanks.

To learn more, on my next business trip to Washington, I visited several prominent national think tanks with different ideological proclivities. I spent most time at the Heritage Foundation, a well-funded conservative operation very interested in influencing national policy. Months before the 1980 presidential election, a group of conservatives advised Heritage to draw up a plan of action for a possible conservative administration in January 1981—to challenge "the past liberal bias of the federal government." They felt that should a conservative win the election, the ten weeks between the election and the presidential inauguration would provide little time to prepare a new governing philosophy and a radical redirection of policy. They'd offer a well-thought-through platform of conservative ideas that could reshape the new administration.

Heritage organized 20 project teams involving 300 participants to develop comprehensive policy recommendations for all the Cabinet departments, and several federal agencies. Each team, with its chair, included some of the best conservative thinkers from academia and past conservative administrations. Their result was a 1,000-plus-page document, "Mandate for Leadership: Policy Management in a Conservative Administration." It was published just as President-elect Ronald Reagan was putting in place his transition team at the end of 1980. Reportedly, by the end of Reagan's first year in office, nearly two-thirds of "Mandate's" more than 2,000 recommendations had been or were being turned into policy. The two large volumes became best sellers. For the 1984 election, Heritage published "Mandate II."

As I thought about this Heritage model being utilized to great effect, I envisaged what might be accomplished were a similar methodology implemented with different values.

Could we establish a new kind of think tank that approached each societal problem using a context of holistic values? What about breaking out of obsolete paradigms, which the university commissions also had been considering but lacked the will to implement, and which High Wind was attempting to do on a small scale?

I mentioned this idea to my former university colleague now in Congress and he was enthusiastic. He said he regularly received Heritage's hard-hitting, well-researched papers on every conceivable issue, and that they arrived at the ideal moment before the debate and voting. Nothing comparable crossed his desk from the progressive corner.

Several weeks later, one of the most thoughtful leaders from Findhorn in Scotland showed up for a few days in Wisconsin. He was very astute, interested in policy, and intrigued with the big question of how to relate the experience of the alternative community movement to mainstream culture. Together, we hit upon the idea of organizing a conference that would address two questions: Was something being learned in alternative communities—the Findhorns, High Winds, and hundreds more—that should be important to the broader society? If so, how could better bridges be built? How to reach the decision-makers?

ODYSSEY
Steps Toward a New Kind of Think Tank

by Belden Paulson

B.J. After describing a possible new breed of politician, in your last column you also began to explain your efforts to create a new kind of think tank. These efforts came out of your participation in several University groups looking at where higher education is going.

Q. How did all this lead to your helping to organize a national conference in New York to create a "New Synthesis Think Tank?" (A continuation of the discussion in the previous column.)

A. Soon after the Findhorn contingent left, Gordon Davidson and Corinne McLaughlin flew out to visit us. They were on a national tour for their new book, *Builders of the Dawn: Community Life-Styles in a Changing World*. As founders of the Sirius community in Massachusetts in 1978 and having previously lived at Findhorn, they were among the most knowledgeable students of communities in America. They had visited and researched 100 intentional communities (including High Wind). They had consulted with governmental agencies and corporations and were familiar with Heritage and other think tanks. One of the key themes in their book: intentional communities are:

*laboratories for researching and testing . . .
components of a new cultural vision . . .*

training places for creative participation in the unfolding of the future. They are schools for change, for transformation.

We all agreed that before planning a conference or considering the more grandiose venture of creating an alternative think tank, we needed a preliminary gathering to examine in depth what we were trying to do. We also invited leaders of the International Center for Integrative Studies (ICIS) in New York, which had contacts with scholars, scientists, business executives, and educators worldwide. Over a two-week period in February 1986, my university department sponsored a seminar in Milwaukee co-hosted by High Wind, Findhorn, Sirius and ICIS on the subject, "Toward an Alternative Think." We invited 40 people from the area including elected officials, business representatives, and civic leaders. What developed was a trenchant dialogue. The conclusion: there is a need for "intermediate structures" that bring together in a new synthesis the best of the mainstream experience of contemporary culture with the best of the new alternative movement. There was recognition of the abundance of knowledge and skills and resources available in today's mainstream society, but there was also recognition of the need for new models and fresh thinking for intractable problems—which were being pioneered by alternative groups.

Gordon and Corinne lined up ideal conference space at the United Nations Plaza across from U.N. headquarters in New York, again co-hosted by our same organizations. They assembled an incredible list of people—a veritable "who's who" cross-section of alternative organizations in the 1970s and 1980s from the landscape of cutting-edge thinking and action in American life. Sixty people came from the media, government, business, academia, as well as from alternative communities and groups.

For the two-day session in October 1987, titled "New Synthesis Think Tank: Laying the Groundwork—An Invitational Dialogue," we sent a letter that began: "We would like to invite you to participate in creating a major new think tank with a select group of influential thinkers and doers. . . . The purpose of the think tank will be to serve as a bridging structure to identify successful holistic ideas and models for mainstream use as potential solutions to current societal problems."

Several of us had written papers on the kinds of problems and projects the New Synthesis Think Tank initiative could address, which were published in a monograph and discussed at the conference. Some were reprinted in *The Forum,* an ICIS magazine whose circulation included a select worldwide audience. I also presented at the conference my own published paper, "Toward a New Kind of Think Tank."

The response from some influential *Forum* readers, including Robert Muller, assistant secretary general of the U.N., and the enthusiasm displayed through the intense dialogue at the conference, convinced us that we had begun an endeavor that could have far-reaching potential.

Lisa and Bel outside Hawthorne House, their new solar home at High Wind
(photograph by Ronald M. Overdahl, reproduced by permission of the *Milwaukee Journal*)

JULY 6, 2010

ODYSSEY
How a Solar House is Born

by Lisa Paulson

Q. You designed and built your solar home at High Wind back in the mid-1980s. Can you tell us how that project was developed, both from a technological and philosophical standpoint?

A. Back then, Hawthorne House was pretty much state-of-the-art. A great deal of research has gone on since that period when people were just beginning to learn about "alternative energy," including building with a passive solar design. ("Passive solar" means no machines or active panels at work—just giving the sun maximum opportunity to shine in.) I'll detail our thinking process and how the construction unfolded, and then will touch on what's come over the horizon more recently.

A primary purpose for establishing the High Wind Association and community in 1977 was to create demonstrations of energy efficient buildings that expressed our concern for preserving and enhancing the environment, and then to bring people in to educate around ecological sensitivity and sustainability in all facets of life.

It wasn't until 1985 that my husband Bel and I could consider building our own home at High Wind, which would join our flagship bioshelter and (eventually) other private dwellings on a high ridge southwest of Plymouth.

Our geography presents interesting challenges. Its 43 degrees latitude makes for winter temperatures that can drop to minus 20 below zero and soar to 100 degrees in summer (though neither extreme is prevalent). Our exposed, high elevation is subject to frequent strong wind velocities. And because our hill slopes east rather than south, it is not considered ideal for solar construction. These factors were key in designing a home that had to work in tandem with nature. Actually, Bel and I came to sit on this hill for years before High Wind began, connecting to this spot of earth and its incumbent natural dwellers. We spent a lot of time examining the natural contours of the site, noting when and where the wind blew, where the snow fell and collected, and how the sun moved (such as seeing what time it disappeared over the west hill on the shortest day of the year). In fact, patterns of light, weather and views (and integrating these with projected social functions for spaces) became the pivotal guiding factors as I began to sketch plans.

Now, when we were ready to build, we had to take into account these and other factors, in a very practical way. I pored over hundreds of articles, books and pictures, researching both design possibilities and the newest technological developments. Our architectural bible became Christopher Alexander's *A Pattern Language*. For Alexander, building becomes poetry, not simply a matter of bricks and mortar. As we proceeded, we began to see our own house unfolding as a partner in a distinctly artistic enterprise with its own personality of grace and beauty and power. We named it Hawthorne House because each spring the hedgerow of tangled wild hawthorne trees on our east flank becomes a cloud of white blossoms.

Many drawings later, we invited in a good friend from Spring Green, Keith Symon, who was not an architect but a fine carpenter/cabinet maker who had designed and built a house we liked, who knew a lot about passive solar, and whose ecological and aesthetic integrity we trusted. It was particularly important to me to prove that a technologically efficient solar house could also be artistically compelling; I wanted it to be lyrical, to "knock your sox off," and at the same time to be understated, warm and inviting. Together, we talked and dreamed and drew; then we modified the more fanciful ideas and scaled down the dimensions to reasonable proportions. In spring 1985 we discovered Peter Paiser, a builder of earth-sheltered homes from Two Rivers who was intrigued at the idea of combining his technologies with others, including passive solar. Between Bel and me, and our designer and builder, we came together on the "final" plan—though we kept it fluid and actually made changes throughout construction.

In order to be part of the constant decision-making and to eyeball the results, I was on-site most of the time serving as general contractor, running for supplies and lining up subcontractors. Correspondence between Keith and me continued briskly since his guidance and overall vision were critical in making everything work together. Often we were in virgin territory, and Pete, on his end, was ingenious at knowing how to resolve complicated construction puzzles or errors with remarkable creativity and speed. Keith appreciated especially that Bel and I were intimately involved with every step of the project; he would not have taken on the assignment if we had tried to turn over the entire responsibility to him and Pete—to be handed the key at the finish.

The bulldozer rolled in to excavate August 1, 1985. Soon the site resembled an archeological dig, with the different levels of earth connected by ladders, and a fascinating geological history was spread out in the open cross-sections. The glacial residue, or moraine, consisted of topsoil, clay, packed round stones, fine pebbles, and beach sand, with the course of a long-ago stream clearly visible. Pete and his crew of one or two apprentices did most of the construction over the next 10 months. (Our son Eric also came to help for a while). I found masons to artistically cut and lay the slate floors and to build the fieldstone hearth (we collected glacial rocks from our own land). We also arranged for other floorings and the active solar hot water system (designed and assembled by a plumbing teacher from a technical college). As snow piled up around me in the partially enclosed building, I sealed the boards for the exterior cedar siding just ahead of the carpenters nailing them on.

I had contacted makers of innovative, energy efficient products all over the country, from low-flush toilets to air-to-air heat exchangers. Because the house would be open indefinitely as a public demonstration, we received a number of substantial discounts and outright donations (including all our water-saving faucets from the nearby Kohler Co.).

The house, being next to a hardwood forest that protects it on the north, is dug into the west hill so that roughly half the building is underground, sheltered from the prevailing winter west winds. The other half of the house is passive solar, exposed to capture the sun and sweeping views over the valley to the east and south. From the beginning, the architecture was dictated by the land, with the house growing organically out of the existing earth contours and giving a feeling of stepping down with the hill. The interior spaces evolved out of this natural flow and from light patterns from the huge triple-glazed windows.

Here, in brief, are the (abbreviated) nuts and bolts describing some of the design specifics and energy features:

House plan: It's 1½ stories and roughly 2,300 square feet. It's "stick-built," double stud construction with poured concrete foundation and berming walls. A sun deck and herb-rock garden are accessed from the dining area on the south. A north-facing screened porch is a cool oasis in summer with views into the woods and over the valley. The primary energy-saving elements in the house are triple-glazed windows, superinsulation, earth-berming, and mass for heat storage.

Upper level: Living room, dining/kitchen area and sunspace/study on the upper level are open-plan to facilitate radiant woodstove heating. The master bedroom and bath are also on this floor. Ceilings vary from a cozy 7 feet to 8 feet when stepping down into the living room. There's a modest cathedral (11 feet) sloping up to clerestory windows over the kitchen to light the darker areas to the north. (You don't want to lose too much heat in a high plenum.)

Lower level (walk-out): A large study, two guest bedrooms, bath, and utility room.

Floors: Where the house is built directly on-grade, there is 4 inches of poured concrete, under ¾-inch slate. Where not on-grade, there is maple or vinyl flooring.

Walls: On the north, west, and east they are 12 inches thick with insulating values of R-56; south walls are R-45 and 6 inches thick. Sprayed urethane (5½ inches) insulates the 12-inch walls; 2-by-4 stud walls have fiberglass insulation.

Roof: Trusses are 18 inches deep with blown-in cellulose for a protective R-60. Asphalt shingles are lapped more tightly than normal to protect the (19) low pitches (ranging from 2½ inches to 12 inches to 6 inches to 12 inches). Roofs on a solar house usually have a 24-inch overhang to keep out a maximum amount of summer sun, but Keith felt we needed every bit of winter sun we could get and it was worth the small inconvenience of a little less summer protection—so our overhangs are 18 inches.

Windows: The key element in our passive solar scheme is letting the sun in directly and retaining its heat as long as possible. Though our degree-days in Wisconsin are 7,000, we do surprisingly well, since the coldest winter days are often sunny. We opted for an abundance of south-facing windows as well as a number on the east to catch morning sun. By opening the fairly small living room with huge windows and setting them 22 inches from the floor, the outdoors becomes an integral part of the room, keeping us in touch with the wild meadow surrounding the house.

All vertical windows are Hurd Heat Mirror, produced in Wisconsin: there are two layers of glass separated by a 1-inch air space, sandwiched with an invisible 2-mil-thick reflective film in the middle. The windows have the "magical" ability to allow direct solar gain into the house by day in winter, but keep 85 percent of radiant heat from escaping back out at night. Conversely, in summer the windows allow in light but keep much of the long wavelengths of heat on the hotter outside of the glass.

Eventually some of the windows failed and their replacements had the newer feature of argon and krypton gas injected between the glass layers. There are two Velux skylights to bring light into strategic spots along with several high clerestory windows.

ODYSSEY
Creating Plymouth Institute for Sustainability

by Belden Paulson

B.J. You reported that the consultation you helped to organize in New York on a new kind of think tank generated enthusiasm for producing enlightened policy-making. I understand it also had repercussions overseas, and led to initiatives in Wisconsin.

Q. Along the way, what did this have to do with creating the Plymouth Institute and its innovative sustainability proposal in Sheboygan County?

A. Only the fickle hand of fate prevented a nationally known think tank and a state-of-the-art ecovillage from being established just outside of the town of Plymouth less than 20 years ago. This initiative began after that consultation in New York.

Some of the 60 consultation participants met informally to discuss next steps. After numerous small sessions, they looked to me to play the lead role for now, in part because I had a base in a university where most think tanks were located; and also because I'd presented a draft of a model. I recruited two astute policy-oriented futurist thinkers to share responsibility. They were Bob Olson of the Institute for Alternative Futures headquartered in Washington, and Wil Kraegel, businessman and futurist in Milwaukee with whom I'd been teaching.

Using a model similar to that of the Heritage Foundation, we agreed to produce 15 terse 10-page policy papers related to the 13 departments of the federal government, plus the Environmental Protection Agency, and the Office of Management and Budget. We'd identify one or two prominent holistic thinkers for each subject whom we'd ask to write a paper or be interviewed. We received abundant advice for preparing our pool of interviewees. In our initial telephone contacts, the three of us found high interest in cooperating, while we were also seeking funding for the project.

Barbara Marx Hubbard, author and lecturer on conscious evolution, belonged to a famous wealthy family. Active in citizen diplomacy efforts with the Soviet Union in these last years of the Cold War, she was intrigued by our think tank initiative. She agreed to participate in a workshop at High Wind in the summer of 1988, also attracting several others with funding capability. Apart from the expanding interest in our admittedly ambitious intentions, she pushed on two other fronts. First, we should change our name from New Synthesis Think Tank (hard to pronounce and too "New Age") to Plymouth Institute—a serious conservative label for a radical idea. Second, she was engaged in organizing an international summit in

Moscow for January 1990: "Restoring the Global Environment: Sustainable Development for the new Millennium." She asked that I chair a task group with a Soviet counterpart: "U.S.-USSR Think Tank on Global Perestroika." One recalls that Communist Party General Secretary Mikhail Gorbachev was pushing his new Perestroika policy of open thinking.

In Moscow, building on the Perestroika and citizen diplomacy background, after two days of animated discussion our 40-member international task group came up with its recommendation: to establish A Global Think Tank for an Interdependent Sustainable Future. Its organizing council would have five members drawn from the U.S., USSR, India, UK and China. Representatives from these nations were all present except China.

That spring I led an American delegation to China to study future trends, which included participation in a Shanghai conference on the interrelationship between the environment and economic development. I ended up co-chairing a workshop there on the global think tank idea. The project marshaled such enthusiasm in Shanghai that one Chinese leader was ready to come to America "to begin." A second visit and conference the following year reinforced this interest.

While a focus on sustainable development and living had been a priority at High Wind from day one, this theme was now going mainstream. In June 1992, the United Nations had convened a world summit in Rio de Janeiro to push its new strategy to save the environment while reducing the rich-poor gap.

It was called "The Three E's": environment, economics, and equity. President Bill Clinton, in one of his early actions after the 1992 election, created the President's Council for Sustainable Development. (High Wind board member Bob Pavlik and I served on its education task force.)

For our Plymouth Institute think tank effort, Olson, Kraegel and I now refocused our work to emphasize sustainability. A local group linked to High Wind and to the UWM seminars that Kraegel and I were teaching, was also generating exciting ideas and proposals. Despite surprising national interest in our project, also reflected by our Moscow and Shanghai experiences, little money was forthcoming. In order to enlist broader university support, apart from my own department, I submitted a proposal to a special university fund to create "Action Learning Labs for New Policy." The plan was to enlist core groups of 25 people in five different Wisconsin communities—to broaden the way people see the world, with specific steps leading to sustainability efforts. The university administration said it was a great idea, but they had no money.

All of this is background for a new kind of pressure we were feeling close to home, which I will describe in my next article.

The Review *cartoon after the ecovillage proposal was rejected.*

JULY 15, 2010

ODYSSEY
Pioneering Ecovillage Plan Developed—
and Then Rejected

by Belden Paulson

B.J. In your last column you described the effort that brought world-class proponents together for a consultation in New York to design a new kind of think tank. This initiative moved to Wisconsin, resulting in a new local entity, an offshoot of High Wind you called Plymouth Institute.

Q. Though the hoped-for backing for an international think tank based around enlightened policies didn't materialize, the new Plymouth Institute plunged into creating a plan that would put Sheboygan County on the map as a pioneer in the relatively new field of sustainability. What can you tell us

about developing the groundbreaking concept of an ecological village and how that turned out?

A. From the start, High Wind had been committed to protect the hills and valleys in its Kettle Moraine sub-region of Sheboygan County from conventional subdivisions and development. Three times when surrounding lands had come up for sale and developers were ready to move in, High Wind had been instrumental in arranging for compatible groups to buy the land. This happened on two different adjacent 20-acre tracts, and also on a large 62-acre parcel.

Thus, when a part of the contiguous 144-acre ecological treasure known as Silver Springs was plotted out for a subdivision, we were concerned. This property was a natural gem, with abundant spring water, forested ridges and wildlife. It boasted one of the noted trout farms in the state. It also included a lodge with restaurant and four luxury chalets that could be used by visitors who came to fish or enjoy the rural ambience. We searched across the country for a sensitive buyer who would protect the property while utilizing the existing facilities. At the last minute, in lieu of any alternative, a small group of High Wind-related associates risked their limited personal resources to buy this unique property themselves.

Our goal was not land investment but to expand High Wind's contribution to sustainable living. After discussion of many plans, including the possibility of using this special setting for a model conference center, we reached the decision to design a state-of-the-art ecovillage. The three purposes: 1) to demonstrate a high-quality example of land use, keeping in mind the unique ecology of the property; 2) to implement the sustainable living ethic, with advanced uses of renewable energy practices and land planning; 3) to generate income to pay off the mortgage so that the land could not once again be prey to conventional developers.

Since this was a complex undertaking requiring specialized knowledge across several fields, a think tank approach was needed. Bil Becker, part of our small High Wind core group, (himself a professor of ecological design at University of Illinois-Chicago, who at one time worked with the visionary architect/inventor, Buckminster Fuller), enlisted Mike Gelick, a noted architect from Chicago with solar experience. He also brought in

John Hinde, an inventive water expert from Illinois. Lisa and I recruited Michael Ogden from Santa Fe, a national expert in designing biological waste treatment systems, using controlled wetlands to eliminate the need for conventional septic systems. Bob Pavlik, also in our core group, (professor of education at Marquette and Cardinal Stritch Universities), worked with Becker and me to develop an education advisory group to use the ecovillage experience for tangible learning demonstrations. Tom Scott, a telecommunications design expert, drew in talent to create a state-of-the-art communication center so that some village residents could work at home. Mel Blanke, a Plymouth-based attorney and High Wind board member, formulated an ecological covenant and structured the project as a land condominium where individual and joint ownership are combined.

Over a couple of years, an ambitious ecovillage vision evolved with the hard work of this talented group. We allocated 70 of the total 144 acres of Silver Springs for the ecovillage itself. There would be 25 units, aesthetically clustered on the high ridge with spectacular views and surrounded by hardwood and pine forests. Homes would be solar, with several designs offered by Gelick, or members could create their own. All homes would link into the "living machine" wetlands technology where human waste is converted into clean water after passing through an array of plants and living organisms. All buyers would own a share of the substantial common land, a wilderness to which they'd all have access. During a naming process, Lisa came up with "SpringLedge." As soon as word leaked out— that we were seeking people "looking for the good life, who want to become land stewards respecting the earth while creating their own nest of extraordinary beauty in a quality environment"—a line of folks showed up as potential buyers.

The Midwest Renewable Energy Association recruited Becker and me for their annual big gathering to lead a discussion on ecovillages, using the SpringLedge example. Plymouth Institute (our new umbrella non-profit entity created for the project) hosted a national conference, "Ecovillages and Neighborhoods," drawing academics and practitioners who told us that our project was one of the most carefully thought-out models they had ever encountered. A luncheon, co-sponsored with *The Review* in Plymouth, brought in John Todd from The New Alchemy Institute, one of America's foremost innovators in ecological design and a colleague of Ogden creating biological waste treatment systems.

On June 5, 1996, Mel Blanke submitted our completed plan to the Mitchell Town Board for approval. According to local ordinances, a sketch plan had to be approved by the board, and then more detailed plans would be provided for final approval. There were architectural sketches for proposed solar homes, and a draft of the condominium declaration. There was detailed material on the waste disposal system, which had been discussed and approved by state and county officials; they were enthusiastic about this model with a lower environmental impact than conventional septic systems. The project would contribute significantly to the local tax base, and with the condo association taking responsibility for plowing and driveway maintenance, there would be minimal demands placed on municipal services.

Usually Mitchell Town Board meetings were sparsely attended, but at this one there was standing room only. Virtually all the people who spoke were against it. They opposed a number of new people moving into the area; they said this might create a voting bloc that would take local control. They said the waste system would never work, and they argued that commonly owned land rather than individual ownership was alien to the local culture. One vocal person complained that High Wind itself did not pay property taxes (the town treasurer refuted this).

The board made no decision to approve our sketches, postponing action to the next monthly meeting. In the interval several of us met with five residents in the town, all opposed to the project. It turned out that they themselves had moved to the township very recently, and now they wanted to close the door to further settlement. At the next town board meeting, the crowd was even bigger. One of the most adamant neighbors stood up to read a petition that he said 80 people had signed to oppose SpringLedge. He asked who in the room approved the petition; almost everyone stood up in favor, except for our small group and a few others. Someone in the meeting pointed a finger at me and suggested that I move to Russia; obviously, anyone who advocated holding land in common must be a communist. Another person voiced a concern that our (one) proposed low-cost building would draw "undesirables" from the city who might bring vandalism and crime to our bucolic neighborhood. At this point, Mel asked to table any decision until the next board meeting.

We were urged to talk to *The Review* and the *Sheboygan Press*. As yet there had been no coverage on what was happening. The newspapers attempted to summarize the arguments of both Plymouth Institute and the opposition. They also discussed the concepts of the ecovillage and sustainability, as well as the environmental and educational work of High Wind and Plymouth Institute.

There was even a description of our own solar house (detailed by Lisa in an upcoming column). While the press comments criticized Plymouth Institute for not having invested more energy in educational work with our Mitchell neighbors (most effort had gone into working out the complex details of the project), the articles and editorials were, by and large, supportive of the ecovillage and also of the contributions of new thinking and models and resources that this initiative would bring to Sheboygan County and the Plymouth area.

Before the next town board meeting, our Plymouth Institute group, at the suggestion of several neighbors, reserved the Town Hall for an informational meeting. A number of us made presentations about project details, including one Sheboygan business leader who was so enthusiastic about the project that he had already put a deposit down on one of the first building sites for his family. The atmosphere with the 50 people in attendance was more civil than the hostile environments of the previous meetings, although I doubt that many opinions changed.

At the next Town Board meeting, again with standing room only, there was no opportunity for discussion. The three board members rejected the ecovillage, and a one-year moratorium was imposed on any new development in Mitchell.

In the next days, a plethora of articles was published on how our work had stimulated the area to think about smart growth and enlightened zoning policy. Editorials in both newspapers emphasized that this whole process served as a wake-up call for new thinking.

Hawthorne House interior (photograph courtesy of Eric Oxendorf)

July 27, 2010

ODYSSEY
The House Just Sits There and Performs Its Magic

by Lisa Paulson

Q. Can you tell us something more about how your solar house at High Wind performs?

A. Last week I described the process of creating such a home. Here is how it worked out for us.

How passive solar works
The purpose of the concrete and masonry floors is to soak up the sun's heat by day and release it slowly during the night. If we've had several bright days to charge up this "storage battery," the effects are enjoyed for a period of cloud cover. The low angle of the winter sun penetrates 15 feet into the living room and hits the massive fieldstone hearth where more heat is absorbed.

Woodstoves: Backup for the solar system consists of two woodstoves, a Jotul #8 in the living room and a Kent downstairs. On the advice of the seller, these do not have catalytic converters (which are tricky and can break easily); ours do well on "garbage" or soft woods. I should emphasize that for the first 11 years we had no central heating—and (I told people proudly) an almost zero fuel bill (we mostly picked up dead wood from our forest). But then Bel and I began to worry about our ability to haul and chop wood as we got older. I researched somewhat environmentally friendly alternatives and came up with the Lenox Complete Heat system: a gas water heater that vents some of the excess heat around the house. It felt almost sinful; I could flip a switch and get almost immediate warmth! Remember, however, that we still needed to resort to propane only when there was a cloudy spell. Just recently (when the Complete Heat failed after many faithful years), we installed a new energy efficient boiler—but again, it's only used when there's been no sun for a while. The woodstoves are still employed but less often.

Other energy-saving technologies: Having gone to great lengths to make the house tight to retain the heat, we had to deal with stale, possibly toxic, air—so we installed an air-to-air heat exchanger that makes for five complete air changes in the whole house every hour (using the outgoing, warm stale air to heat the incoming, fresh cold air).

An active solar domestic hot water system provides nearly 100 percent of our hot water when the sun is shining; on cloudy days, it's now backed up by the boiler.

To protect against further heat loss—from the "glass holes" in the house—the east bedrooms have pocket windows (hollow-core doors cut down) that slide out of the walls to cover the glazing. For years we also used foam board pop-ins.

When we first moved in, we waited to decide on coverings for the large dining and living room windows; we wanted to experience every kind of weather before buying. Actually, we found the need was more to protect ourselves in winter from overheating and glare than from the cold. Especially with the low sun penetrating, we found it difficult to sit comfortably next to the windows; temperatures could shoot up over 85 degrees at the Thanksgiving table with no back-up heat going. We opted for accordion-pleated

blinds that let in a lovely filtered light and stored at the top in only 1½ inches. There is a small R-factor as well when deployed for winter coziness.

There were other energy decisions: We have no dishwasher. Until last year we had no clothes dryer (succumbed to a dryer when our 30-year-old washer quit and had to be replaced, but we still hang out 95 percent of the time).

Coming out of our 24th year here, I continue to be amazed at how we have to strip down to T-shirts when the sun blazes through our Heat Mirror windows, even in the coldest weather. One of the really satisfying things about living in a passive solar house is looking out at mountains of snow glinting under a brilliant sky; it may be February and below zero out there, but in my living room it's 80 degrees. It's also satisfying to know that I'm not using any wood or propane backup. I won't have to light fires later, either, because heat is being stored in the slate floors and hearthstones, and will slowly release during the night. There are no fans or machines to make this happen; the house just sits there and performs its silent magic. And it's gorgeous!

Living in Hawthorne House has been extraordinarily pleasant from nearly every standpoint. I enjoy the opportunity to be sensitive to what's happening outside, fine-tuning the building to work with the natural elements that allow it to take its place among them. And I like sharing information about the house with frequent visitors; High Wind is always on the annual National Solar Homes Tour.

As I said at the beginning, our house was cutting-edge when we built it, but now the advances have galloped way past our modest, pioneering (and relatively cheap to build) experiment. Though we've saved a huge amount on fuel bills, there still is some cost (especially now that we've "given in" to a conventional, though very efficient, boiler).

I invite you to check again the *Review* column of March 23, "Net Zero Energy House Possible." Our next-door neighbor, David Lagerman, discusses their combining two very efficient approaches: a "high mass" system that, with exterior active solar panels, stores heat in 2 feet of sand under the house foundation; and a "downsized geothermal" system that takes heat from the ground in winter, concentrates it and delivers the heat indoors (in summer, working in reverse, heat is pumped out of the house and dumped underground). Installation and operating costs are not trivial, but the outlay may be justified compared to the energy required to run conventional systems.

I'll end with a favorite quote from Christopher Alexander:

> *[There is] a fundamental view of the world; when you build a thing you cannot merely build that thing in isolation, but must also repair the world around it, and within it, so that the larger world at that one place becomes more coherent and more whole, and the thing that you make takes its place in the web of nature, as you make it.*

We did our best to follow this guideline in the adventure of building our house.

ODYSSEY
Schools Can't Go It Alone in Their Communities

by Belden Paulson

B.J. At the beginning of your chapter, "Wake-up Call to the Learning Establishment," you mention a national conference your department organized when economist Robert Theobald discussed the implications of his new book, *The Rapids of Change.* He asked the audience if they thought today's educational system was preparing our youth to cope with the swift currents rocking the world. The people chuckled at such a preposterous question and no hands went up

In your book you write at length about education: organizing efforts with Milwaukee's inner-city students; teaching university seminars on policy issues; helping to found two innovative inner-city public schools; and serving on university commissions grappling with the future of higher education.

Q. Given the high priority of inner city problems in education, what were some of the strategies that you designed with the grassroots leadership and the authorities to improve learning?

A. When the Russians launched Sputnik in 1957 it shook up the educational establishment, stimulating in the 1960s a great debate for educational reform. The prevailing idea was that society was failing because our scientific education was falling behind. The debate has never let up. In 1983 it resulted in the publication "A Nation at Risk," a report of the National Commission on Excellence in Education appointed by the U.S. secretary of education. The commission concluded:

> *If an unfriendly foreign power had attempted to impose on America the mediocre educational performance that exists today, we might well have viewed it as an act of war. As it stands, we have allowed it to happen to ourselves. . . .*

In the following years hundreds of reports have come out for every aspect of school reform. While this movement initially focused on primary and secondary schools, it quickly extended to higher education. It was becoming obvious that the educational establishment was a conservative institution, ill-prepared to match the transformations taking place in our society and the world. In earlier years many articulate individuals voiced new thinking, but later reform efforts were more "official." They involved state boards of education and governors, local school superintendents, major education associations, and professional groups. Naturally, there were interlocking directorates where authors and policy-makers belonged to the same networks using common conceptual frameworks. Despite this huge investment of energy, however, results have been very mixed.

After I joined the university in the early 1960s, some of my main efforts focused on the inner city. A 60-block survey convinced us that the biggest single issue facing the youth was the reading problem. Once kids had fallen behind several grades by junior high school, everything in their lives started to go wrong. We organized pilot programs for reading and eventually established a network of tutorial centers scattered through the inner city, usually operating out of church basements, using mostly volunteers, and cooperating with the university reading clinic. We developed a widely used manual on how to organize a first-rate tutoring program. Over subsequent years, every research study has confirmed the basic importance of reading.

Our next big initiative was to figure out how to build better cooperation between school and community, to overcome the anger and alienation toward authority generally and schools specifically. The tension was intense between inner-city leaders and the conservative public school board—considered unresponsive to community needs. Threat of violence was always present. We organized the Central City Teacher Community Project, where teachers used any legitimate creative way to win the confidence of each kid and motivate the family for learning. At one time this high-impact program reached one-quarter of all Milwaukee inner-city schools.

We trained a couple hundred block leaders who were incredible forces in winning trust. They were expert in identifying community needs that had to be dealt with and gained political support. Although the reading problem and alienation were central to low school achievement, an effective response had to recognize a whole package of factors. This meant training teachers and administrators so that they could reach the child with a relevant curriculum. It meant recognizing the role of a safe and stable home environment and parental support and dealing with single-parent and alcohol and drug issues; noting conditions of physical and mental health, including nutrition; the employment situation and family economic security and the question of whether the child must go out to work at an early age; ability to buy books and wear presentable clothes; the home situation, including sanitation and heating and study space. In essence, school reform really required comprehensive community development, which led to our helping to found the Harambee Revitalization Project and other community development initiatives. It also pushed us to design a "community health" model that viewed "health" in a holistic sense.

It's not surprising that planners of school reform often produce meager results in low-income areas; it's because they conceive the school as a stand-alone entity instead of belonging to the surrounding community infrastructure.

ODYSSEY
School Reform Bogged Down by "The System"

by Belden Paulson

B.J. While our schools in Plymouth and She-boygan County and our post-secondary colleges and vocational institutions are all struggling to offer quality education, there is a huge national challenge facing America: we are losing our competitive edge in the global economy.

Q. What helpful ideas and models emerge from your experience that could offer value for us here and for this great national need?

A. When I offered seminars that generated plenty of ferment in challenging the education status quo, the participating teachers, after momentarily getting excited, frequently came back with two responses. The first: "It's great to be gung ho for change because we all know it's needed, but every person I know already feels stressed, overworked, frustrated." To every new idea, the answer was: "Leave me alone, I can't handle a lot of new learning. Things may not work very well and I may not be terribly successful, but at least I've figured out how to function and survive in my own way. . . ."

The second response: "Even when I feel good with what I do, I may come across an idea or model that appears better than mine. I might be open to give it a try. But I know the *system* is not going to change. With all

the rules and regulations, the teachers union, the school board, the monolithic layers of bureaucracy, the budget crunch, not to mention all the needs directly tied to student poverty and dysfunctional family backgrounds—whatever I do in my classroom is not going to change the system. The bottom line: change in education is not going to happen."

Notwithstanding this pessimism, my colleagues and I have always found teachers and administrators and community leaders willing to stick their necks out to seek a better future. As of 2007, the U.S. is number 12 in the world in percentage of adults with a college degree. It's reported that fewer than 25 percent of 2010 high school graduates taking the ACT college entrance exam have the academic skills necessary to pass entry-level college courses. When we organize "summits" of concerned people open to investing extra time in facing these negative trends, they immediately agree on three points: 1) a paradigm shift is going to happen in education sooner or later because it has to—the alternative is too scary to contemplate; 2) because most people will not buy in, we must find teachers and principals and parents and schools and civic leaders willing to take risks; 3) to get operational, we must mobilize talent and find the best models and *do something*.

In this and two subsequent columns I'll cite three examples, very briefly, from personal experience of "doing something." These are discussed in detail in my book. One of the pioneering models about new thinking about learning is Waldorf education. It is not "new" because this was conceptualized in the 1920s and 1930s by one of the 20th century's seminal thinkers, Rudolph Steiner, a radical Austrian social thinker born in 1861. There are more than 500 Waldorf schools worldwide, including more than 100 in the U.S., with several in Wisconsin. Because Waldorf education stresses the interplay between the student's inner experience and the outer world, its curriculum interrelates culture and history and the humanities with the physical world of nature and science. In developing profound concepts about the process of how people learn, Steiner formulated his model of a threefold image of the human being's faculties: *thinking*, *feeling*, and *willing*. These qualities are cultivated at different rates as a person evolves from infancy into adulthood, each stage with its own learning requirements. Because Steiner was heavily influenced by the tragedy of World War I and the Russian revolution and the rise of Hitler, his philosophy was oriented toward social and spiritual renewal, a need as urgent today as when he lived. Waldorf graduates tend not only to perform exceptionally well academically; they also face life with an idealist aptitude for service.

One active participant in my seminars in the latter 1970s was Mark Stamm, who subsequently trained to become a Waldorf teacher. After working elsewhere, he returned to Milwaukee and convinced the superintendent of Milwaukee Public Schools (MPS) about the value of Waldorf education. In 1990 the School Board approved establishing a Waldorf school in Milwaukee. Since until then all Waldorf schools in America were private, and were located in areas drawing more affluent students, this new "Urban Waldorf School" pioneered on two fronts: It was the country's first *public* Waldorf School, and also the first to be located in the inner city, drawing mostly lower income and minority students. Mark and the schools recruited me to organize an intensive university training program for the first cadre of teachers.

After the superintendent left MPS, some system staff raised doubts about the radical Waldorf approach to education; they said it was "too far out of the mainstream for Milwaukee." In this model, for example, the same teacher accompanies the same class of children through all the elementary years, and is responsible for all the main subjects (with specialists for foreign language, crafts and physical education). When questions arose, I helped to assure that the school would be implemented and funded.

Urban Waldorf became well known nationally, as did our three-year training curriculum. Academic performance and attendance were exceptional, and observers arrived from all over the country. However, recently MPS lost its enthusiasm for this radical model and just this year, after 20 years, the school was defunded.

Two private Waldorf schools in metropolitan Milwaukee continue to prosper, but I'm aware of no comparable initiatives in Sheboygan County, although now and then people have expressed interest.

ODYSSEY
Innovative School Ideas Tend to Die on the Vine

by Belden Paulson

Q. Continuing the discussion of problems in our schools, are there other ideas and models that came out of your experience, which could offer help for us locally and for our national need?

A. A second example in personal experience of "doing something" is the promising initiative to create global citizens in MPS. The seed for this initiative was planted after I returned from leading a study trip to China in the early 1990s. While moving around China, I was regularly being asked if I knew Americans who would like to come work for a year or more to teach English and help Chinese youth learn something about our culture.

Once home, I discussed this with the MPS deputy superintendent. Why not set up a pilot program, let's say begin with 100 students, to prepare them as "citizens of the world"? He was enthusiastic and we drafted a paper: "A School for Global Citizenship—Working and Living in the 21st Century."

A colleague and I offered two seminars on this idea through UWM, and another professor did a comparable course through Cardinal Stritch University. Several MPS teachers and administrators also enrolled. Out of these seminars emerged a draft blueprint. Once the deputy became superintendent, he worked with us to establish a task force involving several innovative school officials and parents. We designed a small pilot school titled the Global Learning Center (GLC), approved and funded by the school board, and beginning operations in fall 1998.

While our model had many innovations, its most dramatic feature was to base learning not in a traditional school building but in six interconnected "cluster centers" scattered around the city, each with unique characteristics (e.g. the Milwaukee Art Center, the Schooner Project attached to the port where a tall ship was being constructed, the downtown UWM campus, etc.). Each cluster had a learning coordinator, and one or two learning mentors (who had college degrees but were not certified teachers), plus volunteer parents. Four certified teachers moved around as core staff. One of the administrators who had taken our seminar served as "principal" (but more as lead teacher). Each student family signed a learning agreement, and there was heavy parent support.

The first several years the GLC was extraordinarily successful, with almost perfect attendance (most students were recruited from the inner city) and above-average academic achievement. Then the enthusiastic superintendent and a couple of key school board members retired. The MPS planning department did not like the school because the initiative originated from the outside the system; the teachers union did not appreciate the unorthodox staffing arrangement; and the MPS building and grounds department never accepted this model of not using a traditional school building (notwithstanding much reduced costs).

After five years, the GLC was defunded, although there was a push to convert the program into a charter school and to utilize the model. I understand that international education and student exchanges have expanded in recent years in our area schools, a welcome trend.

These first two examples illustrate, in my view, the kinds of "out-of-the-box" thinking that the educational enterprise desperately needs. They point out the importance of creative leadership, but also the essential role of "staying power" so that good ideas and models will be sustained over time.

Unhappily, creative individual leadership in education appears so scarce that when visionary officials leave the scene, the prevailing institutional mediocrity and the lethargy of traditional bureaucracy reassert themselves. New thinking dies on the vine before it can take hold long term. The literature is full of brilliant ideas and promising pilot models, which do not fundamentally change educational structures and behaviors because the sparks that are lit peter out too soon.

The 1984 Living/Learning seminar meets during their first community stay—at High Wind

SEPTEMBER 9, 2010

ODYSSEY
Living/Learning Schools Create
Life-Changing Experiences

by Belden Paulson

Q. Let us have a final example, now, of an innovative educational idea that came from your own experience, and which could be relevant in the conversation about changes and reform in learning practices.

A. My third example, although small-scale, produced positive long-run outcomes. It grew out of the seminars held each summer at our High Wind intentional community located seven miles southwest of Plymouth. We would invite about 20 participants from all over the country to live for a week or two at High Wind. Each morning we offered an

intellectual experience with several speakers, in the larger context of utilizing effective experience that has been shown to work while also welcoming new transformative ideas. The rest of the day they would work with community residents in construction, gardening, and other hands-on projects. Underlying the experience was the challenge of actively preparing participants to build a sustainable world.

In 1979 Lisa took a group of 23, of all ages, on a two-month study trip to Findhorn, the world-famous intentional community in northern Scotland, which was developing a real-world model for a sustainable lifestyle. Since virtually everyone who participated in the High Wind and Findhorn programs had positive experiences but complained that they were too short, the obvious answer was to create a longer, more comprehensive model. We labeled this the "Three-Community Living/Learning Seminar." Besides Findhorn, we invited other intentional communities, such as Sirius in Massachusetts and Eourres in the French Alps to be part of this experiment. I got the university to approve a full semester, three-month offering, providing full undergraduate or graduate credit. Seminarians lived for one month at High Wind, one month at Sirius or Eourres, and one month at Findhorn, followed by a few days back at High Wind to evaluate the whole experience. They participated fully in the life and work of each community, with substantive discussions on major themes dealing with community life as well as the state of the world. They created their own smaller community while living in the surrounding larger one, practicing the same approaches to personal interactions, problem solving, and decision-making they were observing in the larger context. There were no traditional exams, but each person kept a daily log, and at the end of the program, wrote a comprehensive paper on what they had learned.

When I had participated in various university commissions to reform higher education, certain planks surfaced regularly: Students must be prepared to become global citizens; curricula must break out of narrow departmental confines to cross disciplines; learning must be experiential with real-world value beyond the claustrophobic classroom; values and societal concerns must be integrated into the cut-and-dried process of transmitting knowledge. Our Three-Community seminar attempted to incorporate all of these themes.

Our first project was in fall 1984, with 12 participants, including two from Sheboygan County, two others from Milwaukee, three from California, two from the East Coast, one from Kansas, and two from Canada. They were all in their twenties except for a married couple in their thirties. They wrote incredible papers on the experiences of their group, with reflections on the three communities visited, on what it takes to build a sustainable world, and above all on their own learning to become more fulfilled human beings. Most had life-changing experiences.

A research project is now underway to determine what impact this experience had after looking back 25 years. We sponsored five more of these seminars, until travel costs proved prohibitive. I consider these programs among my most significant in 35 years of university teaching.

I've often thought that one or more schools or colleges in our Plymouth/Sheboygan region could make a significant contribution by organizing a *School for Sustainable Living*. This could build on some of those models and experiences to prepare our youth and creatively contribute to the great educational enterprise, sorely in need of help.

ODYSSEY
"Intentional Community" Described in
An Unconventional Journey

by Barry Johanson

Lisa Paulson is co-founder of High Wind, an experimental community near Plymouth. In her book, *An Unconventional Journey: The Story of High Wind, from Vision to Community to Eco-Neighborhood* she gives voice to the nearly universal yearning for connection that people are feeling today. In the face of increasing hardships on many fronts, we feel an urgency to join together for mutual support to satisfy our material and psychological needs. We yearn for the sense of safety and solidarity that feeling part of a community offers.

Author Paulson not only documents the development of High Wind, an experimental "intentional community" southwest of Plymouth in the town of Mitchell, but she also describes the related attempts of groups through the ages to create more workable societal strategies.

From early on, Paulson has looked beyond the mainstream and felt compelled to challenge status quo trends and values. She sees the imperative for different cultures to stand thoughtfully in each other's shoes. She recognizes that a sustainable way of life is best realized in the cooperation of groups such as "intentional communities"—relatively manageable entities whose members try to live out a particular vision.

In *An Unconventional Journey,* Paulson captures the accomplishments and the disappointments, the successes and the challenges, of living as part of an intentional community. Through words, as well as through 27 annotated photo spreads, she tells the story of her own unconventional journey that resulted in the creation of High Wind, the development of this unique community, and the lessons that can be learned from it.

The book will initially be available at Book Heads in Plymouth. Paulson also is a contributor to *The Review* with her husband Belden, as authors of the "Odyssey" series of columns.

ODYSSEY
How Can a Young Person Make a Difference?

by Belden Paulson with Judith Pintar

B.J. Halfway through your book, after having detailed your experiences overseas addressing horrific poverty in the slums of Naples, finding solutions for some of postwar Europe's most difficult-to-resettle refugees, working with the United Nations, consulting as an expert on international communism, and then joining the University of Wisconsin to teach political science, design economic development research in drought-ridden Northeast Brazil, and create a new department to confront urban poverty and racism, you make a rather startling revelation. You write, using the date of the end of 1978:

> *I was beginning to realize I was no longer the same person who'd been walking this earth . . . I was undergoing my own personal revolution—or using a more accurate word, "transformation."*

Your wife Lisa had recently returned from Findhorn, the renowned spiritual community in Scotland. She experienced profound personal changes there, and then you, too, traveled to Scotland. You met world-class thinkers articulating a "New Age." You then organized a series of new university classes and also national conferences on subjects considered "alternative" to the traditional curricula. They dealt with the environmental crisis before it surfaced in the mainstream, as well as sustainable lifestyles for the coming post-petro age, and above all they re-examined and pushed our values toward a more compassionate society.

Then you and Lisa and your associates created the nonprofit High Wind Association "to develop a sharing community where people live together in cooperation with one another and nature. . . ." High Wind received a grant from the U.S. Department of Energy to build a model solar building. Over the next two decades, a residential community coalesced to live on the land near Plymouth, and the organization attracted hundreds of people from all over to attend its programs and tours, and to visit its alternative bookstore in Milwaukee.

Q. Years later, the High Wind board of directors conducted a survey of people who had lived in the community or participated in some way in its programs, including classes sponsored with the university. The goal: to assess what influence High Wind really had on peoples' lives. What did you learn?

A. Since we were continually running into people from our orbit of activity (including some from this area), we identified 180 of those who had been most involved locally, from across the country, and from overseas. We asked them to complete a very comprehensive questionnaire. The 60 who responded provided a mountain of data. Bob Pavlik, of our High Wind board, tallied the fascinating, sometimes lengthy comments in the open-ended questions. All the material is summarized in my book, *Odyssey of a Practical Visionary*, and could, itself, constitute a small book.

Overall, we were impressed with the laudatory comments. One observation was made again and again: *It is important that High Wind exists. America needs you.*

While this is not to overlook the critiques, the responses reminded me of a thought I sometimes had on the role of monasteries in the centuries that historians refer to as the Dark Ages (the thousand years from the fall of the Roman Empire to the Renaissance). It's not necessarily that the monasteries were perfect, but they did stand for something. Within the context of all the human failings around them, they articulated and tried to live a visible idealism the world needed.

For this column I'm focusing on just one respondent. Judith Pintar attached two extra pages to her questionnaire. While still a senior in high school, and then as a college student in the latter 1970s, she enrolled in all of our early seminars, leading up to the creation of High Wind. She joined the first group we organized for a study trip to Findhorn, and later went back. She visited High Wind many times as it evolved but was never a resident. We considered her a kind of prodigy, always a lively participant with a fertile mind. At a young age she learned to play the Celtic harp, composing, performing and recording her own music. She wrote books and poetry, and became a storyteller in the schools—all in her early twenties. Later, she married and earned a Ph.D. at the University of Illinois where she taught sociology. When she went to Bosnia—then in the throes of chaos—to research her dissertation, she identified deeply with the dire conditions and misery of displaced people. She did field research in post-war Croatia, a study that focused on the effects of collective violence and the ways in which traumatized communities heal.

Judith recognized the value of the High Wind experiences for her own life in her youth, over 25 years earlier. But she also had some second thoughts about the idealism and optimism of New Age thinking that was prominent in that period (the latter 1970s and early 1980s). She raised cogent questions about the distinction and interrelationship between individual change or transformation and changing or transforming the larger society. In that period the Cold War was still with us and there was the ever-present fear of a nuclear blowout. There were also vivid memories of big-city social chaos and riots. She asked: Since the New Age movement of that period was mostly attracting the white middle class and focusing on "self-actualization," what did the Findhorns and High Winds have to do with the need for fundamental social change? Which raised the question: Where should a person or an institution invest primary energy?

Certainly society had to deal with these big problems. But Judith felt the New Age movement of that period was most interested in raising individual consciousness. It meant people working on themselves to achieve personal balance and to make full use of their own talents, not necessarily serving the world. She questioned whether the Findhorns and High Winds had anything to do with the urgent need for true social revolution. Today this would mean dealing with climate change, poverty and racism, dysfunctional politics, reforming education, and so on. So what should an idealistic, concerned person, who wants to make a difference, do?

Many young people here in our Plymouth and Sheboygan region are facing the same great challenge: *What should I do with my life?*

The New Age movement that Judith was immersed in has generally dropped below the radar (and those of us who were in that camp 30 years ago dislike being associated with that term because it has become so distorted and diluted), but today there are myriad activities where one *can* invest one's energy.

In my next column Judith shares her thoughts on these issues.

Indian drumming at High Wind (Judith facing, in dark shirt)

NOVEMBER 30, 2010

ODYSSEY
We Only Changed Ourselves

by Belden Paulson with Judith Pintar

B.J. Five years ago High Wind conducted a survey of people who had participated in some of its programs. They were asked what effect the experience had had on their thinking and lives. Continuing from the last column, here is more of how Judith Pintar responded.

J.P. We were so hopeful. I think we recognized all the positive signs in politics and culture as evidence that the New Age was upon us. . . . The New Age was a movement of cultural and economic elites, mostly middle-class and white, whose interest was mainly on personal growth and self-actualization, and that ignored issues of poverty, racism, and social inequality. . . .

I think the problem was that we were mesmerized by the possibility that individualistic solutions might actually be able to address and even ameliorate social (and global) problems. . . . There was always talk of Transformation, and very little in the way of Revolution. Our path was Spirit, not Politics. High Wind was a righteous place that served as a beacon, a haven, a way-station. I have no doubt the community and the organization was a powerful, positive influence on many people, just as it was for me. I would not be who I am without the years I spent as part of the High Wind circle of folks. The values of the community and environmental sustainability that High

Wind championed have never lost their power and salience.

If there was a "deficiency," it was not in the project of High Wind itself but in the larger vision and spiritual movement that High Wind was part of . . . Put simply, we didn't have a plan for getting the rest of the world to create realities that looked like ours. We didn't come up with a strategy for turning our ideas into a social movement. . . .

If I could "do over" the last quarter century, I would invent a different New Age movement, one that recognized that those in power create the realities for everybody else, until people take that power away from them. We should have been fielding political candidates from minute one. This movement would have put economic justice front and center . . . I wish we had been part of a social movement that had more political and popular appeal.

If I am honest, I have to say that I didn't want that then. I wanted to retreat into utopia with other likeminded people. I wanted to work on myself and still feel I was making a positive contribution to the world. I see now that that was naive, but I think I had to go through that time to get me to this one. I really didn't want to be a sociologist then, but I have to be one now.

B.P. "Perceptive, powerful stuff," I wrote in my book. Sometime later I replied to Judith, saying I felt exactly the same way when working in the caves and ruins of Naples. Anything less than a radical social/economic/political movement was useless. (The communists were trying to do this, but they had their own limitations.)

I felt the same in Northeast Brazil where a small, insensitive political elite had locked in place the miserable status quo and nothing short of political revolution would change anything. Sometimes I entertained the same thought when dealing with the impervious bureaucracy in the university or the public schools; the needs seemed so obvious that nothing would change without some sort of major upheaval.

Like Judith, I'm convinced of the importance of political action and eradicating inequality. The question is how to go about it. In essence, I'm convinced it always comes back to the need for good people. Amazing things happen to improve the human condition when the actors involved embody certain values, whether the action is on a large national or even global scale—or even small, as in one's own family.

When one examines the many revolutions and upheavals through history, there were the very beneficial ones and also the disastrous ones. The key determinant for me was the quality of the people engaged.

My original contact with Findhorn convinced me that what that community represented seemed to contribute more to this process of transformation than did the other institutions I knew. Judith seemed to conclude that the Findhorns and High Winds (in simple terms, those trying to actualize a New Age) were naive, and yet that contact prepared her for her current responsibilities and leadership.

Q. Judith, what are your current thoughts on these issues?

A. Five years after filling out Bel's questionnaire, I still agree with my essential critique of the "New Age" vision, which looked toward an evolution for all of humanity, but which was unconscious of the narrowness of its appeal. There wasn't much room for meat-eating smokers in our imagined future, you might say. Unfortunately, because we couldn't find a way to be relevant to the working classes in America, we left them vulnerable to the increasingly canny manipulations of other political agendas. I really don't know why it didn't occur to us to be more class conscious or politically active in the late'70s and early '80s, except that we truly believed that personal transformation of enough individuals would inevitably lead to a social transformation of culture and institutions, somehow without a fight. I didn't think in social terms at all when I was part of High Wind. The plain good sense of living in an environmentally responsible way, recognizing the negative impact that humanity has had on the planet, for example, was self-evident. It was impossible for me to imagine at that time that anti-environmentalism could become a populist cause.

Studying the wars that attended the breakup of the former Yugoslavia as a graduate student in the 1990s radically changed my worldview. As I witnessed the power of political and religious ideologies in shaping people's realities (beliefs, fears, and actions), I understood that political, corporate, and religious leaders will deploy propaganda through the media, mercilessly sacrificing ordinary people's lives to maintain their power and enrich themselves. It was a short step from there to the realization that social inequality is not an unintentional or accidental condition, but that extreme prosperity for some requires extreme poverty for others.

What to do about systemic and entrenched inequalities, both local and global, is the key question, which Bel seems to have arrived at too, full circle. Neither of us has an easy answer. It is a question for young people to take up now, since increasing the inequality between rich and poor across the planet is a destabilizing force that will affect every aspect of their lives for the rest of their lives.

The shortcomings of spiritual philosophies and political strategies aside, there are two aspects of High Wind, the commitment to environmental sustainability and to intentional community, that I believe are as important and relevant to the present and future as they were 30 years ago. As the earth's population grows, and environmental pressures increase, High Wind's bioshelter project seems prescient. The experience of intentional community living that High Wind explored also strikes me as ahead of its time. My husband, sociologist David Hopping, and I are involved with an organization that studies the theoretical and practical possibilities of "community as intervention." One example of this is Hope Meadows in Rantoul, Illinois, a multi-generational, multi-racial neighborhood that supports families that have adopted children from foster care (see: http://www.generationsofhope.org/).

I would not have understood the significance and social potential of this intentional community, when we moved to Illinois to go to graduate school, had I not grown up and lived through the early years of High Wind. Personal transformation was not the only thing that we were about in those early years in Plymouth. Both High Wind and Findhorn placed great emphasis on the quality of our relationships—between ourselves and the earth, and between ourselves and each other. It is neither naïve nor overly optimistic to suggest that transforming our social relations can lead to the transformation of the social world. It's not inevitable, there's always opposition, but as a sociologist I have seen, in practice, that it's possible.

ODYSSEY
Survival Means Finding the Balance
Between Competition and Cooperation

by Belden Paulson

Just after I finished my column on dysfunctional politics that you requested, there was a remarkable turn of events. In short order, our government actually functioned. Congress passed three significant pieces of legislation, all signed by the president: maintaining the Bush-era tax cuts for two more years plus additional middle and lower income-oriented subsidies; repealing the ban on known gays and lesbians serving in the military; and ratifying a new strategic arms agreement with Russia.

This broke open the long period of gridlock and partisan jockeying that has prevented our government from confronting urgent issues, and which resulted in a historic turnaround in the mid-term elections.

I remember years ago, just after college, the period when I was working face-to-face with homeless, starving cave dwellers in bombed-out postwar Naples. I returned home to enter grad school at the University of Chicago. At that time its political science department was rated one of the best in the world. I was urgently looking for answers to my burning questions about how to prevent more "Naples disasters" in the world.

I got a lot from courses taught by one of the most eminent political scientists, Hans Morgenthau. But as I wrote in my memoir, *Odyssey of a Practical Visionary,* what I was looking for was not there. Morgenthau's basic thesis, articulated in his classic *Politics Among Nations,* was that given the very nature of human beings, we must expect their constant quest for power. If idealism or morality is voiced in world affairs, this is usually a cover-up in the struggle for power. I shared my frustration with one of the brightest senior doctoral students. His recommendation: "Read everything Morgenthau has written, take all his courses, then go talk to him. That's what grad school is all about: know your professors, challenge them, then work out your own ideas." Years later, Morgenthau and I have maintained friendly dialogue. He applauded my international experience and I respected his realism.

What Morgenthau taught his students, as did many other political scientists, is that politics is inherently dysfunctional if it is primarily expected to be a means for solving problems. This is because *the essence of politics is competition*—the struggle for allocation of scarce resources that will benefit the interests of particular individuals and groups. In contrast, the essence of problem solving is *cooperation*—the need to create a community of interest where people work together for a common good.

When the political system appears to be functioning, this means that the cooperative impulse is working equally well or better than the competitive drive. Pursuit of the larger common interests of the local community or the nation overcomes the more narrow, self-serving interests of individuals, groups and political parties. It's a delicate balance. There is a natural built-in tension between the realism espoused by Morgenthau in the struggle for power and the push to cultivate cooperation to solve problems. The greater the stakes and the more complex the problems, the more difficult is the challenge to find formulae where the larger good will prevail over narrower interests.

If self-serving interests overwhelm all efforts to seek the common good, the result may not only be dysfunctionality, but anarchy. This can lead to failed states (e.g., Somalia, et al), or even complete collapse (eloquently described by Arnold Toynbee in his monumental *A Study of History*, noting the rise and fall of nations and civilizations). At the other extreme, it's also possible that there is a seeming "common interest" created that initially appears to serve the public, but in reality is controlled by a small group, ending up in the same self-serving way. This time it manifests as a dictatorship. (Hitler, at the beginning was welcomed in post-WW I Germany and won elections.) In short, some healthy tension is desirable between the competitive and cooperative drives, so long as the long-run net result serves the larger public interest.

In today's America, many of us are aware that dysfunctional politics have almost paralyzed our national leaders, preventing them from resolving urgent problems. Let's cite several:

• **The Debt.** Everyone is discussing the need to cut government spending and reduce the huge deficit. So here's what we have recently agreed to: holding on to all the Bush-era tax cuts estimated to cost at least $4 trillion over the next decade, and then adding more. President Obama established a bipartisan commission that just issued its final report. It calls for a $100 billion slash in defense spending; a gradual gas tax increase of 15 cents; pushing the social security age to 69 by 2050; chopping the federal work force by 10 percent; reducing farm subsidies by $3 billion; scrapping big mortgage deductions. With huge opposition already mounting, will it happen? The fundamental question: Can the push for cooperation to serve the larger national interest overcome all the competitive vested interests?

• **The Jobless.** Since the recession with its stream of massive layoffs, the official unemployment rate is now 9.8 percent of the labor force, and close to double that if all the under-employed are included. While each month the statistics are eagerly awaited to deal with this immediate situation, there's a fundamental long-run problem hardly being addressed as yet by the politicians: there's glaring evidence that we no longer need our total labor force. With modern technology, ever-increasing productivity, and exodus of jobs through globalization, this was the conclusion of a national conference I helped to organize in the 1980s. Addressing "The Changing Role of Work," a nucleus of corporate, union, government and academic leaders recognized that new models must be devised to distribute the ever-increasing national wealth without the total labor force. At the same time we must provide for social equity, and we have to find new ways to utilize the talents of our population. Given the political dynamite that this problem encompasses, it's a great test for an enlightened leadership.

- **Poverty.** The official number of poor in America is now 44 million, more than at any time in the 51 years of the count. This doesn't include the uncounted homeless, young adults who are still at home, and some of the working poor who can barely cover necessities. An ominous danger is the increasing income inequality. The evidence: from World War II to 1976 some 10 percent of the population took home less than a third of the income made in the private economy, but in subsequent years the big winners have been the well-off. In 2007 the top one percent of households pocketed 23 percent of national income. The losers are not only the stereotyped inner city single mothers on welfare. Many who had held good-paying jobs now have declining incomes, or they've been laid off altogether. Further, there's a close correlation between educational achievement and income level. But our educational system is in need of massive reforms; a recent international survey affirmed that the comparative state of American education is getting worse. Among 30 developed nations, the U.S. is now 21st, 23rd and 25th, respectively, in science, reading, and math. Now, with the chronic deficit problem necessitating the shrinking of programs, the structural long-run problem of employment, and the accelerating inequity of incomes, we are overdue for creative leadership to confront these issues.

- **Sustainability.** In my view, the most pressing need, apart from issues of war and peace that faces all of us, including the policy makers, is to build a sustainable world. This means that as we fulfill our own needs we must also not compromise the opportunity of future generations to fulfill their needs. There's more and more evidence that we're using up the natural capital that sustains us—water, minerals, oil, trees, fish, soil, air, and the living systems such as grasslands, wetlands, rain forests, wildlife, species diversity. Furthermore, we're facing the threat of climate change that could alter the planet's ecological footprint. It's obvious that we need to rethink how we see the world. It's not only a physical and economic problem. It will require a shift in perception, with changes in our habits and lifestyles. The years are passing, the trends are getting worse, and our political leaders are still mired in narrow partisan bickering, unable to deal with this extremely complex matrix of issues.

In my last column I noted that Judith Pintar, a precocious teenager, was involved in past years with New Age-type activities, including in her early years participating in the spiritual community, Findhorn, in Scotland, as well as the High Wind eco-community in rural Plymouth, Wisconsin. In her "youthful innocence," Judith was introduced to a world "that could be." She saw her early experiences as "a beacon, a haven, a way-station," as she put it. Sometime later she became immersed in the chaos and violence of Bosnia while doing research for her doctorate. She realized that the world of idealism she had experienced earlier was inadequate. Politics had to be the answer. I felt exactly the same way after the stark realities of Naples.

So I studied political science with eminent professors like Hans Morgenthau.

I have no regrets at all about my years preparing to be a political scientist. At the same time, I have no misgivings about the subsequent years I spent helping to organize High Wind and taking scores of students to Findhorn for life-changing experiences. Americans today desperately need preparation for the political process—the competitive give and take of how decisions are made to allocate resources. But they also desperately need the imagination of a world "that could be." They need to be nurtured with the "big picture" values of compassion, empowerment and justice represented by the Findhorn/High Wind models.

The question: *Can our dysfunctional politics be transformed into functional politics, into governance that really works because we've found the magic formula for integrating competition and cooperation?*

This is the great challenge.

ODYSSEY
An Evolution of Idealism: Reflections on High Wind

by Lisa Paulson

B.J. Lisa, recapping what you last wrote about High Wind, you described how the community was conceived—in a rush of idealism in the late 1970s, a time when a few people were beginning to question the long-accepted beliefs and ways of mainstream culture. How they worried about the endangered ecological systems. How they were listening to the ominous rumbles that all might not be well with the generally accepted economic model of growth and competition. While this minority was picking up subtle warning signs that priorities and values were skewing, you noted that most people tended to look the other way. They jumped on the consumerist train that promised the moon: a bigger house, fancier gadgets, jobs that would pay for all this. They thought scientists would surely be able to invent ways out of environmental and energy problems, and that experts could assure an ongoing, healthy economy. Both you and Bel have explained in these columns how the High Wind experiment came into being specifically to address these crises, and how the community grew and flourished.

Q. What happened with High Wind eventually? What is going on now?

A. Thirty-five years ago, the little group that started High Wind had seen the trouble looming for the planet, for our civilization. We believed there were ways to address the trends, or at least to start the ball rolling. We decided to create a small demonstration by changing the way we ourselves thought and lived and acted.

Those of us who came to initiate the High Wind community—with its experimental "bioshelter" and solar homes, its example of a simplified, low-consumption lifestyle, and its innovative educational offerings, discovered two things.

First, we found that there was a real hunger out there for our prescient, future-oriented ideas. People were coming from frenetic urban lives to soak up the healing ambience of High Wind's 128 peaceful acres southwest of Plymouth. They came to hear about a new awareness that had to do with making sure that not only people, but also all life forms on earth must be respected and protected if all of us are to thrive and, indeed, even survive.

Visitors began to hear about High Wind in the nearby metropolitan areas, and then across the country, and even overseas. Growing numbers came to learn and to dialogue about the impending dangers and to brainstorm with us.

The second thing we noticed: At the same time that we were attracting these potential cultural game changers, we were also gaining visibility in our local area. High Wind was a bunch of heterogeneous, mostly young folks in their 20s and 30s (Bel and I were nearly a generation older)—a demographic that stood out by itself in the midst of a traditional farming township. We were advocating a novel kind of home construction employing renewable energy, and radical ways of growing healthy food. We urged restraint in spending habits when most people around us were going in the opposite direction. We were seen as different, a bit strange, and even a threat to a comfortable, familiar way of life. Bear in mind that this was the 1980s, when the economy was booming and before it was generally known that the environment was degrading in alarming ways.

During the 12 years when High Wind was a close, residential enclave—until the early 1990s—crowds were showing up on our doorstep clamoring for programs on every sort of topic, or petitioning to join the community. It was a time of high energy for all of us living at High Wind as our offerings grew exponentially, and we ourselves were clarifying ways to innovate and conserve. As individuals we acquired new skill sets, not least of which was how to work together effectively in close quarters. Our visitors were telling us that even if they couldn't emulate the more aware, responsible lifestyle they saw us taking a stab at, just the fact that we were here, bringing fresh ideas to light, was important and inspiring. Many of them did take the ideas, and they reported back on insights they'd gained and major shifts they were incorporating into their lives.

At the same time that our guest programs were burgeoning and the numbers of supporters multiplying, this caused increasing strain on our small residential group. As unpaid volunteers, the members had to handle not only their ballooning day-to-day obligations, but also had to figure out how to personally stay afloat financially.

We knew that we'd bought into uphill struggles, but felt that because we were breaking new ground, pioneering new concepts, including new societal patterns and standards that called for radical shifts in habits and lifestyles, we had to accept that all this came with the territory.

The result, though, was that members became overloaded and burned out. The simplified, tranquil life we had envisioned and were dedicated to creating and demonstrating, was somehow slipping away.

With this reality, in May 1991 the High Wind board, along with the residents, took a look at what was happening, and made the decision to let go of our identity as an intentional community. The tight-knit group that had adhered to a rhythm of working, living, eating, and strategizing together opted to relax the intensity and pressure this was causing. We decided to think of ourselves, instead, as an "ecological neighborhood" of good friends who still shared the basic High Wind values, but where the heavy, constant obligations were eliminated. We gave ourselves breathing room to exercise our individuality, pursue personal interests and projects, and to enjoy the privacy that wasn't possible before. Those of us who had built our own solar houses continued to contribute time and resources to help maintain the public buildings, to pay the bills, and to plug into the larger vision by interacting with our broader constituency.

Jan Masaros, living in her geodesic dome, used her extensive computer skills to help me lay out our journal, *Windwatch*. David Lagerman kept an eye on the upkeep of the buildings with their quirky technologies that only he understood, and continued to invent energy-efficient devices. Don Mueller continued to cut the trails through our meadows and woods. Bel continued organizing educational programs, often co-sponsored with the university, and I spent time networking and meeting with those on our wavelength who made contact.

We recognized that our 128 acres fell logically into four areas of use: residential (for private homes and personal enterprises); education (programs and retreats in the public buildings—the bioshelter and farmhouse/barn complex); farming (what became Springdale Farm—perhaps the first CSA in the Midwest—where currently some 800 families receive naturally grown food on a subscription basis on 25 acres that former community members Peter and Bernadette Seely bought from High Wind); and conservation (land we set aside to keep wild).

In 1992, an energetic new group of educators from Wisconsin and Illinois, including Bel and me, purchased the adjacent Silver Springs trout farm, an ecological treasure of springs and artesian wells that we vowed to save from development. We created a new entity, Plymouth Institute, and soon obtained a grant from the Milwaukee Public School System to bring 700 inner-city middle school kids up to the land in small groups over the next several years. The young people had a unique opportunity not only to experience being out in the countryside, but were introduced to the important aspects of solar energy, aquaculture, organic farming and nature study. They stayed for up to four days at a time, sleeping in our big High Wind barn. A highlight of this program: The colonel commanding the Wisconsin Air National Guard brought his team of instructors to High Wind, pitched tents for kids and guardsmen (and women), and taught survival skills in our woods. Their stay culminated when the regional general landed in our field in a huge Blackhawk helicopter, met by kids waving flags they had designed and marching proudly in short-order drill. We (peace-loving High Wind!) had been skeptical about bringing in the military, but it proved to be one of our most successful programs ever.

The teaching was superb and the kids ate it up. (This part of our history, including the plan to create SpringLedge, a state-of-the-art ecological village, was described by Bel in an earlier column.)

ODYSSEY
The Community in Retrospect

by Lisa Paulson

B.J. Last time you summed up the creation and evolution of the High Wind community, and how eventually the very acclaim and increased intensity of the work were beginning to wear down the residents. You needed to stop and rethink your future direction.

Q. What were your next steps?

A. In 1998 we had to dissolve Plymouth Institute, and we relinquished the Silver Springs property (most of which, happily, was acquired by the Department of Natural Resources). Members of the Plymouth Institute board joined with High Wind's board, bringing new resolve and vigor back up the hill to "the mother ship." Since we had always been focused on the exchange of ideas, we were next inspired to create the High Wind Learning Center. We wanted to strengthen our central purposes on all fronts: community design strategies, technologies appropriate for the coming age, innovative curricula, and awareness of the sacred. Above all, we were intent on articulating and promoting a new paradigm that would point the way to a viable future as the waning of the petroleum age approached. A busy schedule of events carried on for the next several years.

High Wind Books, the store we had created in 1984, played a major role in bringing alternative materials to metropolitan Milwaukee. Located near UWM, it served as a potent regional watering hole for new thinking. Sixteen years later, in 2000, we sold the store when we could no longer compete with the big chains. Borders and Barnes & Noble began offering the same books we had carried, and soon they were stocking many more than our little shop could hold. We weren't disappointed since we had accomplished exactly what we'd set out to do: we had introduced topics and materials that were new to the area. We had succeeded in raising consciousness in a whole new geographical sector, and had created a link to what we were doing 50 miles north in Plymouth.

Then in 2001, the High Wind board again took stock of our situation and realized that over some 25 years we had achieved the goals we had set for ourselves: to create a viable intentional community, to demonstrate what it means to "live lightly" on the earth, and, together with our buildings and experimental technologies, to show that we had gone a fair distance toward actualizing "sustainability." We sensed it was now time for a change. There was a unanimous decision to sell our High Wind public buildings.

We began looking for suitable buyers who held the same general values as High Wind and would respect and cherish the land as we did. It was our great good fortune to find two Buddhist groups, both of whom had been organizing retreats and classes at High Wind for years, and who knew and loved the property. A Tibetan Shambhala group from Milwaukee bought the bioshelter, renaming it "Windhorse." Japanese Zen practitioners from Chicago became owners of the original farmhouse/barn/chicken coop complex, calling themselves "Bright Dawn."

With cash in hand from these sales, High Wind created a foundation to begin to give away small amounts of money throughout the region. It was a real switch for us, since for nearly 30 years we had always had our hand out looking for donations to stay afloat. We've given grants to Camp Anokijig on Little Elkhart Lake, to the Interfaith Council of Milwaukee, to nature programs for the Milwaukee Public Schools through the Urban Ecology Center, to a Fair Trade business, and to several churches and environmental groups agreeing to initiate sustainable improvements.

Those still living at High Wind (some 20 residents, almost the same number as lived here in our peak community days) continue to coexist gracefully, sharing occasional potlucks, books, DVDs, good conversation, walks in the woods, in-house concerts. A number of us connect actively in the Plymouth community, as well as in Milwaukee.

With our personal responsibility for the day-to-day activities and welfare of High Wind eliminated or greatly reduced, Bel and I have been freed up to write retrospective accounts of our lives and our involvement with High Wind from our different perspectives. My first book, in 2008, *Voices From a Sacred Land: Images and Evocations,* draws on the intimate experiences of all of us High Wind residents living in close proximity to

nature through the seasons and years. Then Bel wrote his memoir in 2009: *Odyssey of a Practical Visionary,* detailing adventures that ranged from resettling refugees after World War II in Italy, to tackling inner-city problems of poverty and racism in Milwaukee to, finally, changing from being a political science professor to a "futurist" looking at long-range solutions for a world in crisis, ending with a detailed history of High Wind. My second book is just out: *An Unconventional Journey: The Story of High Wind, from Vision to Community to Eco-Neighborhood.* This covers my own life journey that led to our founding High Wind, complete with many photos of our life and activities as the community evolved from the late 1970s to the present.

In retrospect, what do I take away from my High Wind experience, probably the major enterprise of my life? I'll quote or paraphrase from a chapter in my book, titled: "Would You Live in Community Again?" This was one of the questions we posed in an extensive survey sent to folks in 2005 who had either lived at High Wind or had participated frequently in our programs.

My answer

It was an incredible experience—from its buildup and preparation from 1976 to 1981 and then through some twelve more years of intense togetherness. We were a very earnest, idealistic little group committed to living the experiment, to attempt modeling a more honest, more conscious, "clean" way of living than we felt we were seeing in the world at large.

At various times, there was both exhilaration and terrible pain, successes and gratifying public recognition, as well as personal and collective dark periods with false starts and stumbles. There was often an excruciating flashlight shone on each of our foibles and missteps—and then the wonderful, close friendships and just plain fun as we labored shoulder to shoulder and knew we were breaking new ground in this corner of Sheboygan County.

It was quite wonderful and even amazing to look back and realize that I had stuck it out and could feel positive about the whole experience. I knew it had been valuable, important. I think most of the others in the community felt the same.

I can't exactly say what I'd do differently if I were to do it again. As some have noted, with all the stumbling toward creating something good and worthwhile, in the end it was really "perfect." The joys *and* the pain. It was a glorious way to learn and to point others on a path of awareness too. But, frankly, I wouldn't have the stamina to try it again, not for myself anyway.

Perhaps a better model would be a less rigidly structured regime with more viability or longevity. An "in-between structure"—maybe some kind of cohousing where people would own their own dwellings in a community complex (more deliberately planned for mutual support than a conventional subdivision). Where they would hold outside jobs for financial autonomy, but where they also could participate voluntarily in periodic shared meals and activities.

All of us often remark that we wouldn't be the close group still living at High Wind if we hadn't gone through the "bath of fire" together. We'd be just a bunch of exurbanites living in energy efficient houses in the same vicinity. We had shared a lot and that remains a precious bond.

Bel and Lisa's mountain house in Vermont that their son volunteered to build

FEBRUARY 22, 2011

ODYSSEY
Eric Built his Parents a Warm House in an Icy Winter

by Eric Paulson

B. J. After many memorable visits to the state of Vermont, you and Lisa finally decided to buy a bit of the land you'd both grown to love. You'd find an acre or two where you could pitch a tent or maybe put up a shack. Purely by chance, in summer of 2000 you came upon a spectacular tract of steep meadowland. It looked out at the White Mountains of New Hampshire, and moose and bear roamed its thick forests. The property hadn't yet been placed on the market, but it was exactly what you had dreamed of; you bought it on the spot. As part of a conservation land trust, its per-acre cost was modest. On returning home to Wisconsin, your son Eric (from the Spring Green area) volunteered to build you a house out there. Since he'd never done this, and

he'd have to build in the ferocious Vermont winter (his landscaping business occupied him in warmer seasons), you all recognized the challenge. Now we've asked him to add to this part of your story from his perspective.

Q. Eric, in your father's book, Odyssey of a Practical Visionary, *it's recounted that early on, even before you could bring in a generator for your power tools, you and your two colleagues began the framing illuminated only by headlamps. There were tales of spectators lining the road at night, wondering who was crazy enough to work past midnight, and in bitter cold and often snowstorms. Tell us about your adventure.*

A. About 10 years ago my good friend, John Reeves, and I built a house in Vermont for my parents, Lisa and Belden Paulson. They asked me to add some of my thoughts and colorful recollections to that chapter in our lives. Because we were building through the dead of a snowy Vermont winter and neither John nor I had built a house before, the stage was set—perhaps less of a project, and more for a "journey."

Having sketched out house plans back in Wisconsin around the dining room table with various family members and friends, John and I packed our tools into two pickup trucks and drove to Vermont in late October. Somehow, my mom was able to find and line up most of the backwoods contractors from a thousand miles away by tapping her growing Vermont grapevine, and by the time we arrived the excavation and foundation were done.

John and I met with the local lumber-yard people, made sure our house plans were structurally sound, and set up the first lumber delivery. We readied the support cast (plumbers, electrician, heating guy and drywallers) for that critical moment when their skills would be required. In particular, we hit it off with the drywallers from New Hampshire. Their state motto was "Live Free or Die," words they lived by. And though we came from opposite ends of the political spectrum, these erudite community activists engaged us for days in an ongoing Socratic dialogue about everything from the way a government should run, to Joseph Campbell's mythic realities, to carpentry details we needed advice on.

This was fairly typical of all the local trades people. They were informed, opinionated and talkative. In uniquely Vermont fashion, the local dowser, with forked stick in hand, accurately located the well, and

he also never hesitated to throw in his two cents on any subject. Last but not least, in our building triumvirate was Branislav (we called him Brian) whom we brought out from Wisconsin to provide some extra man-power for framing. Only a year away from his native Czechoslovakia, he proved to be a quick study and way too cultured to be on our crew, but a great addition.

We impressed upon everybody involved that timing was important. We couldn't stick around the area for years finishing this house, as is the custom in rural Vermont. Amazingly, people took us seriously. Being "from away" (out-of-towners) didn't hurt. Our reputation for shoveling a foot of fresh snow before a day's work and then working into the night by generator lights produced stories told back to us by lumberyard personnel who got a kick out of our earnest style. And it was useful that they took a shine to us with our strange antics because every few days we had engineering questions that needed to be answered before we could proceed, or there was a special order to be given priority. It seemed that everybody wanted us to succeed.

So we were making progress. With the truss floor installed and the exterior walls all pushed up, John, Brian and I were standing around one day looking at drawings for our next phase, the roof trusses. As John and Brian looked up from the blueprints, they were astonished because it seemed as though I'd suddenly vanished into thin air. I was as surprised as they were because I had taken a step back and plunged down through the hole cut for an eventual stairway, descending one story below to the basement floor. I landed on my feet, brushed off my momentary shock, climbed back up and we resumed our discussion.

Then, only a couple of days later, we were up in the rafters nailing down roof trusses.

John was high on a ladder, tools in both hands, when he slipped. It so happened that John sported a pretty healthy beard at the time, and he claims his beard caught on a rung of the ladder to save him. Ouch! We immediately remembered my dad's dream from a week before in which he saw Brian get badly injured. We promptly took Brian off high climbing duties, started taking a few more precautions, and got through the rest of the project without incident.

Occasionally, to take a break from the routine, the three of us would drive up to nearby Montpelier in the evening to eat at the Culinary Institute of America, also known as the CIA. It's a national training ground for chefs and restaurateurs. Brian, a bit of a connoisseur himself, was never shy about sending back his entrée, telling the cooks it needed a touch of this seasoning, or the steak should be rarer, etc. Though 25 years old and the least skilled of any of us as a carpenter, Brian was unafraid to keep John and me in line and seemed to have a sophistication and sense of command well beyond his years.

Frequently, John and I would drive the 15 miles or so to the lumberyard to get supplies, and once snow covered the landscape, the almost continuous downhill drive on gravel roads to Bradford was like a slalom course. Usually, I would drive and John, often a bit sleep-deprived, would nap during the trip. To lie down, he wouldn't wear his seatbelt but insisted that if we started to slither off the road into some ravine, I was to quickly get him to buckle in. He was expert at conducting such precise activity out of a dead sleep. We only had to go through that routine twice and never did end up in the ditch.

I have come to realize over my 50-some years that very often the important stuff that happens is not what you've planned or what you think you've accomplished. Yes, we built this house and it was quite an undertaking. But the real storyline, I think, took place below the surface.

It was about designing a house on a paper napkin; and about pulling together a motley crew of backwoods craftspeople, not to mention ourselves, to create a thing of beauty. It's about solidifying relationships and about creating for my parents, particularly my mom, a place where she could bond again with the Vermont countryside where she had spent formative and joy-filled years in her 20s. And it's about all the unforgettable experiences like the ones I'm sharing here that bring a project to life.

Often when I do something for others, my parents in this case, it is I who receive the most. I learned about the power of a project to manifest smoothly when a strong intention is shared by so many, galvanizing parts of ourselves we didn't even know we had. It was about giving something back to my parents who have given me so much. It was about knowing when those times come, to offer your unique brand of service, be ready to act, to step into that moment of appropriateness and make the contribution only you can make.

Addendum (or Afterword) by Lisa

After reading Eric's account, I remembered a few additional incidents in the building process that he had left out or may have forgotten. For instance, in anticipation of the rugged conditions awaiting the building team, John decided to "harden off" by sleeping in his tent pitched in the snow.

Then, as construction got underway and the three guys were working long into the night, sometimes in a swirling blizzard with winds howling, a neighbor would take pity on those "wild men" and bring by thermoses of hot soup. Bel and I visited at one point in the dead of winter and nearly expired after spending just a couple of hours on the as yet unenclosed site; but the intrepid three thought nothing of putting in 12 hours with weather raging around them in below zero temperatures.

In order to sink the posts for the deck into the frozen ground, the guys had to light fires to melt the ice and snow. How often do you hear about that?!

When they got to the finishing construction stages, they brought in professional drywallers who remarked that they'd never come across a house built so absolutely square as this one was. High praise for novice builders! The whole house reflects the meticulous care and artistic ingenuity that our team brought to the project. Now, for three months each year, we continue to absorb the vibe that clearly says this was a labor of love, given with much joy and humor, which shown all through those harrowing, demanding winter months. Ten years later, Bel and I are still filled with delight and gratitude and awe.

Thousands flood Capitol in Madison to protest the curtailing of educators' power

MARCH 3, 2011

ODYSSEY
Dysfunctional Politics at Work in Madison

by Belden Paulson

B.J. In your book, *Odyssey of a Practical Visionary,* you cite many personal experiences in different parts of the world where you faced "dysfunctional politics." Political leaders seemed to prefer gridlock to working together for the larger good. They absolutely opposed considering any position other than their own—"It's my way or no way."

Q. Last week you reported visiting your family in Madison, and described spending a morning at the state Capitol. You joined the multitude of protesters of all ages who were waving signs of every size and description and chanting "Hear our voices!" They filled every inch of the rotunda inside the Capitol building, while thousands of others jammed the streets and marched around Capitol Square. You also found the airwaves saturated with pronouncements by the governor and politicians in the legislature, debating the governor's budget-repair bill to confront Wisconsin's deficit problem. This drama has been going on for many days now. From your years of experience, what did you learn that might apply to this conflict in Madison?

A. Whatever one's partisan persuasion, most of us would favor *functional politics* where we solve problems, as opposed to the *dysfunctional politics* of political paralysis. Several weeks ago I devoted one of these columns to this subject. It may have relevance for what's happening in Madison now.

Eminent political scientists argue that given the very nature of human beings, the essence of politics is competition—the constant struggle for power and for resources that will benefit the interests of particular individuals, groups and parties. Often this is inherently dysfunctional and results in gridlock. In contrast, a cooperative approach (functional politics) is essential for getting problems resolved. People create a community of interest, working together for a common, long-run good that is larger than their fragmented competitive interests.

A classic book, *Founding Fathers,* about America's 18th century revolutionary generation, discusses the ominous threat of gridlock that faced the framers of the U.S. Constitution. They absolutely could not agree on the one great issue of the day: slavery. The southern states, represented by slaveholders George Washington and Thomas Jefferson from Virginia, were poles apart from more northern states; John Adams and Benjamin Franklin were vocal abolitionists. Finally, both sides had to compromise on the vital goal of saving the Constitution for the larger good. Slavery was not resolved until the Civil War, a century later.

In my book I discuss my contacts with the Communist Party in Italy in the 1950s and 1960s when the communists were close to taking over the country at the height of the Cold War. Since they made clear that they alone held "the truth," there was no basis for bargaining about anything. My friend Athos Ricci who, as local Party secretary, had helped make his village the most communist-voting in all of Italy, and when I met him, had just left the Party. He told me that the Party's claim of existing only to eliminate poverty was completely false. Their real goal was to win national power. Athos

subsequently helped to bring more give-and-take into local politics.

When doing social science research in Northeast Brazil with a Brazilian university in the late 1960s, my group was attacked by a vehemently anti-American political party. These far leftists assumed that all Americans in the area were working for the CIA and were not interested in advancing local development. There was no reason to sit down with me and my colleagues to understand our work. Finally, Wanda, a radical young Brazilian woman on our team, risked her own neck by standing up in the public square to vouch for the quality of our research and for me personally. Wanda's speech became the key to opening up a dialogue.

In spring of 1989 when co-leading a University of Wisconsin study tour in China, I arrived in Beijing just as a million students were occupying Tiananmen Square. While discussing the right to demonstrate for political freedom with several Chinese students, I was about to be arrested by a plain-clothes detective, but our local leader, very frightened, immediately evacuated our group. Subsequently, a prestigious institute of Chinese foreign policy experts met with us for a surprisingly frank discussion. They asked how we would deal with the protests, and we offered a variety of opinions. Some of us thought the government actions were justified (this was before the tanks rolled), while others were clearly supportive of the demonstrators. All of us—Chinese and Americans—were grateful that we could discuss this openly and respect each other.

Returning to Madison, the citizens of Wisconsin and political leaders of both parties are agreed that Wisconsin faces a serious debt problem that must be confronted. The governor's budget-repair bill deals with the

$137 million shortfall for the year ending this coming June. There's an estimated $3.1 billion deficit in the subsequent two-year budget cycle, although reportedly the state faced a $6 billion deficit two years ago for the 2009-11 budget cycle. Governor Jim Doyle brought reductions by part-time furloughs of state workers, utilizing one-time federal stimulus money, corporate taxes, and other measures. With the recession officially finished, state revenue was also up. Obviously, functional politics requires that our political leaders find some way to cooperate to pass legislation that deals with the debt.

The governor's budget bill calls for public employees to pay at least 12 percent of their health coverage and nearly 6 percent of their pension. The public employees and Democratic Party legislators have gone on record to accept the governor's proposal for these cuts. Thus, the immediate issue of finding the money in the governor's proposal has presumably been moving in the right direction.

The real roadblock preventing passage of the governor's bill is his desire to strip most of the rights of public employees to bargain collectively, except for wages. Now an extraordinary coalition of publicly funded employees on state, county and municipal levels has come together—teachers, nurses, firefighters, police. They are vigorously resisting giving up their right to organize to protect their work conditions and their livelihoods. Since Wisconsin is known historically as the originator of collective organizing for public employees, other parts of the U.S. are watching intently to see what will happen.

Because this legislation is a fiscal bill, Wisconsin requires that 20 state senators be present to vote. There are 19 Republican senators, but all 14 Democrats have left Wisconsin and apparently have no intention of returning until there is some give-and-take on the collective bargaining issue. (It should be noted that a respected national Republican commentator, David Brooks, has indicated that Governor Walker should be more flexible on this point.) But thus far the governor and the Republican senators have stood firm, with no interest in negotiating, and the Democratic senators apparently are committed to not showing up until the governor's bill is changed. Classic dysfunctional politics!

While the issue at hand is important for Wisconsin, there are some bigger stakes that affect not only our state but the whole country. America's union movement is in serious trouble. In 2010 the number of wage and salary workers who were members of a union had dwindled to 11.9 percent compared to 20.1 percent in 1983 and a much larger percentage earlier. Public unions are what remain of the once-formidable union movement; 36.2 percent of public sector workers are unionized. It's known that in the decades after World War II, unions played major roles in helping workers increase their incomes and improve working conditions. Along with the G.I. Bill, these were critical forces in expanding the middle class and advancing national educational levels.

Some people are convinced that the governor's budget-repair bill is less about debt than a raw power play to disempower unions. It is not by chance that the conservative Koch brothers used some of their billions to help Scott Walker get elected, along with many others, and have vigorously supported anti-union efforts across the country. (Now it's said they're financing the plethora of ads favoring the governor and his budget bill.) Since most unions tend to favor the Democratic Party, and probably have more money to spend than any other electoral bloc, this anti-union work is in reality a political strategy. From this perspective, the current stalemate in Madison may be dysfunctional for legislating, but its essence is the time-honored competitive struggle for power.

A recent *Atlantic* magazine article, "The Rise of the New Ruling Class," confirms much other research that a perilous gap has developed in America between the rich and everyone else. It notes one credible study that between 2002 and 2004, 65 percent of all income growth went to the top 1 percent of the population. The plutocrats are increasingly seen as not only running Wall Street but also running our government at different levels. In this context, what now is happening in Madison is simply one small chapter in what may be changing America. There is urgent need for empowerment in the broader community—local and national—to prevent plutocrats or anyone else from taking over.

In my early paragraphs, I offered several examples where the stalemate of dysfunctional politics has been opened up in the direction of functional politics. Some or all of the following actions may come into play: 1) certain individuals stand up with the courage to break the logjam (in Madison, one or more Republican and Democratic senators could begin negotiations for give-and-take compromise); 2) the notion sinks in that no one has the sole truth (in Madison, some humility on both sides, and recognition of real motives could do wonders); 3) short-term solutions may be necessary for immediate problem-solving, postponing larger, more complicated problem-solving (in Madison, the big issues of dealing with debt and with unions will require more input); 4) the conflict and stalemate may be useful in mobilizing popular interest and clarifying the real issues (in Madison, the viability of the political process for problem-solving in the longer term needs much more work).

Residents of all ages cook dinner together in the community kitchen

MARCH 10, 2011

We Tried to Walk the Talk

by Lisa Paulson

Q. You and Bel have indicated that maybe it's time to wind down your long-running column. Is there anything you'd still like to discuss?

A. Since this is probably our last Odyssey chapter, I want to wrap up my end of it by first saying how much I've appreciated the opportunity to share our experiences and thoughts in this column.

Over the past year, I've written about many adventures—both in my personal life and in creating an ecological community (High Wind being the culmination of a life of testing new ideas, of questioning conventional beliefs and behaviors). It's interesting to note that 30 years ago our ideas at High Wind were considered radical and perhaps

even suspect. First of all, some local people were uneasy about the fact that High Wind was a heterogeneous, residential group (of mostly young people) who had moved here from outside the area. Then they saw we were taking a hard look at some of the mainstream ways things had always been done—which included such basics as how people built their homes and grew their food.

On 128 acres southwest of Plymouth, we built solar houses and grew vegetables without chemicals. With our many visitors and workshop participants, we warned that no longer could we take our energy sources for granted. There were discussions about how humans are only one part of the grand, interconnected scheme of nature, and that it behooves us to respect and cooperate with *all* aspects of creation, of life. In light of the ominous beginning signs of climate change, we discussed the necessity of turning more rapidly to renewable energy and living more responsibly and sustainably. The High Wind folks were looking at the broad picture of how our society was moving: we questioned the way we were being urged to borrow, spend, *consume*. Competitiveness and power seemed to be the driving forces behind economic and political endeavors—and we were opting for alternative approaches.

We chose to showcase a better way of life through the solidarity and commitment of being a *group*—a small but critical mass walking the talk, trying to be an example. We saw our experiment as one way to spell out the urgency of the problems, to attract notice socially and politically, to nudge a larger society that in some respects seemed to be asleep or unaware.

Checking the broader view, I see a bit of an analogy of what High Wind espoused with what's happening presently in the Mideast Arab nations. A vanguard of idealists over there are passionately envisioning a different culture and world and aren't afraid to take the first pioneering steps in this direction. Similarly, in the late 1970s, our earnest little High Wind band was willing to risk livelihoods and reputations by embracing avant-garde ideas and reinforcing values they saw as essential for the very survival of our culture. They went all out to fulfill that dream.

Likewise, in Cairo we saw the impact of growing numbers of people banding together to achieve a new freedom. The movement in Egypt was bolstered by frustrated young people who were pushing against the system—the status quo—as were we at High Wind. Today, with our tightened economy and with natural resources more clearly threatened, the idea of frugality is back into fashion. We're delighted to find that many of our neighbors in Mitchell and Plymouth are joining us now in agreeing that we need to simplify lifestyles and conserve energy.

We were committed to trying out communal living and working in close quarters for an intense period of a dozen years. But in the early 1990s, after that "bath of fire," we also began to see the need to balance our lofty goals with an equally important need for privacy and individual freedom of expression. Even so, nearly 20 years after the decision to let go of the "intentional" aspect of the High Wind community, our values remain strong. We live our own independent lives in our little eco-neighborhood on the edge of the Kettle Moraine State Forest, but "the good of the whole" is always in the forefront of our awareness.

I would welcome the opportunity to dialogue with *Review* readers about anything Bel and I have introduced in our columns over this past year. It looks as though we're in for "interesting times" ahead, and it's up to us in our various communities—our families, townships, counties and country (and on our lands)—to look hard and truly at what we need to do to ensure a safe and fulfilling future for all the inhabitants of these concentric community circles.

Thanks much for this chance to connect with folks in Plymouth and Sheboygan County. It's been a grand ride!

It takes cooperation to get things done

ODYSSEY
Six Building Blocks for a Better World

by Belden Paulson

B.J. It's been an interesting ride this past year—our dialogue about your books.

Q. As we look back, do you have some final thoughts?

A. A year ago, as publisher of this award-winning small-town newspaper, you contacted me. You had in hand my newly published book, *Odyssey of a Practical Visionary.* Your proposal: "I'll pick out a person or event from your book and ask a question or two. In your response, while elaborating on particular subjects in the book, I'll ask you to relate them, when possible, to practical insights about some of today's big issues."

Over the past year, our ongoing "correspondence" ended up as 47 columns in *The Review.* Since my wife, Lisa, had recently published two books—*Voices From a Sacred Land,* and *An Unconventional Journey: The Story of High Wind*—she also contributed articles. Occasionally, other people participated as well, including our sons Steve and Eric, and Judith Pintar, a wise young woman with a keen sense of social and political history.

A few examples of the columns come to mind. I assessed the Haiti earthquake, using my own experiences in war-destroyed Europe when providing relief to people existing in caves and ruins, and observing effective ways to administer aid. Through finding out-of-the-box solutions, I detailed an experiment to resettle hard-core refugees who authorities argued could never leave the Italian camps.

I described a political research project in Northeast Brazil where intense anti-American elements labeled the work as CIA-related espionage, but we saved the project through winning strong local support. I recounted almost being arrested when a million students occupied China's Tiananman Square, but subsequently was involved in candid give-and-take dialogue with Chinese futurists. I wrote about exploring ways to fix our schools that didn't work by creating brand-new models. I explained how a disempowered inner-city neighborhood was mobilized by trained block workers. I noted how teaching futures studies and envisioning a new think tank could push alternative thinking into higher education and traditional politics. And I detailed how ideas for sustainable living were demonstrated and taught by the High Wind eco-community we founded near Plymouth.

I'll admit I had no intention of writing a book. Since I'd experienced a life full of adventures spanning the last half of the 20th century, I simply wanted to write a long letter about these to my four grandchildren, which some day they might take a look at. Perhaps after I'd checked out, they'd wonder: What was our grandfather like in the prime of his life? And how did he get Lisa to live more or less happily with him for more than 50 years?

I had stored hundreds of old letters and documents for possible use some day, and when friends and colleagues learned about this "long letter" I was cobbling together, they asked to see a copy. My final product ended up at well over a thousand pages, but with sifting and prodding by editors, we reduced it to about 750 published pages.

While I probed many challenging problem areas, the thread that seemed to unite the diverse projects had something to do with actions dedicated to building a better world. Notwithstanding many twists and turns, I never did quite fathom the mysterious forces at work whereby each key juncture in my life seemed to lead naturally to the next one. And although the individual projects reflected a great diversity, in a deeper sense they were not that diverse; they all focused on solving problems of human need. They also tended to be "exploratory"; they attacked problems that often lay in unknown territory. Further, when the economic and political strategies normally employed proved inadequate, a nebulous quality I've called "spirit" contributed an essential ingredient.

We have a longtime friend, Henry Halsted, who formerly helped to run the Johnson Foundation's Wingspread conference center in Racine. He had served on the front lines in World War II and saw combat in ferocious battles. At the war's end, with other Allied soldiers, he entered the concentration camps where mostly Jews had been exterminated. Recently, he put together two incredible volumes describing these experiences. His comment upon seeing the Auschwitz camp: "The road to Auschwitz was built by hate but paved with indifference." His point was that the Germans, historically an enlightened and cultured people, had closed their eyes to a hideous situation and allowed it to get out of control during the rise and reign of Hitler. When they might have taken responsibility for what was happening, they slept. When desperate tasks required taking risks, a few answered the call, but too many remained silent, often grasping opportunities for personal benefit or safety.

The great 18th century conservative observer Edmund Burke comes to mind. He wrote: "All that is necessary for the triumph of evil is that good men do nothing." With so many needs and problems "out there," today the question before each of us is how to use whatever talents we're equipped with, mobilizing our energies so that we are not the ones who do nothing.

The stories in the three books by Lisa and me contain large or small episodes in which we, and our many colleagues over the years, galvanized our energies and resources to confront urgent needs. Although I've encountered a lot of grim conditions (people living on the margin of life in several parts of the world, including our own country), I've not had to deal with what Halsted faced at Auschwitz. Nor what the 50 Japanese workers at the Fukushima Daiichi Nuclear Power Station are now faced with: braving radiation exposure and fire to prevent a broader nuclear catastrophe.

For all of us who in our own ways are at work as world-builders, I like to return to a particular set of values. Some years ago I offered a university seminar that addressed the question: What would a sustainable community or world look like? Six very dedicated students got so deeply engaged that they asked to continue for another month after the formal class ended. One product of our joint labor was to agree on a values model so basic that it seemed to transcend all cultural and political differences. It grew out of the image of a holistic society where instead of each of us pursuing our own narrow self-interest in the struggle to survive, together, we learned to see ourselves as integral parts of the larger community. This might be a local area such as Plymouth or Milwaukee but some day it might also encompass the whole world.

Because in various talks and other classes I've found surprising resonance with these concepts, I include them in this series of articles, always keeping in mind my gratitude to Barry and Christie Johanson and their co-workers for our year-long "conversation" together, as revealed in this quite impressive newspaper.

These are the values my seminar and I agreed on that would underlie a sustainable culture:

Cooperation: Interrelationships where the parts of the whole work together for the common good;

Empowerment: Each part gives strength to the others, thus all benefiting with a "win-win" result;

Compassion: Each part extends open arms to the others, giving without expectation of a particular return, thereby creating an underlying trust in the viability of the overall system, even though some participants may be perceived as contributing more than others;

Long-term perspective: Each part places its needs of the moment into a time continuum that far extends its own existence;

Global outlook: Each part sees fulfillment of its own needs in the larger context of the Earth and Humanity;

Sustainability: In sum, sustainability gathers up all these values and implies "the Good Life," where each part cooperates and empowers, interacts with compassion and a long-term perspective, and is globally oriented.

It was agreed that the most important of these single values was Compassion.

Microhydro workshop at Silver Springs, the base of Plymouth Institute

SEPTEMBER 24, 2012

ODYSSEY
Now Is the Time to Rethink the World

by Belden Paulson

B.J. Now, as we near the November 6 elections, the conventions are over but the big problems remain. Only the final chapter awaits us—the question of who will win.

Q. Apart from that question, as a political scientist, what can you say briefly so that whatever happens, America wins?

A. Today's America is unsustainable. We spend more than we have. So we could face fiscal disaster. We're not providing jobs to keep up with an expanding work force. So we could face a labor market disaster. We're using up our natural resources faster than we're renewing them. So we could face ecological disaster.

However, we can be somewhat optimistic because people of all stripes hunger for a vision of the future that goes beyond waffling and gridlock. They truly want to see an America that is sustainable. There's a fundamental urge to regain our "can do" spirit. Our survival as a viable country and world leader is on the line. There are still partisans who believe that only *they* have the truth—there is no give and take. But most Americans know better.

All sides agree that we must drastically cut the deficit.

All sides emphatically agree that we must deal with joblessness.

Most of us, if not all, see the glaciers melting, temperatures rising, some resources running out. The perils of climate change and limited resources have to be confronted.

Where to begin? We need to think short-run *and* long run. On the immediate scene, there's one policy that our political leaders of both parties are talking about. All four candidates—Romney and Ryan, Obama and Biden—mentioned it in their convention speeches: The Simpson-Bowles deficit blueprint.

We recall that in early 2011 the president established a bipartisan 18-member debt panel co-chaired by ex-Republican senator Alan Simpson and former Democratic leader Erskine Bowles. Their final report in December 2011 promised to reduce $4 trillion of the deficit by 2020, and to cut popular programs of domestic spending and the military. It would also raise revenue by ending the Bush tax cuts for the wealthy, and other revenue measures including, possibly, a tax on carbon emissions. Other groups have refined the recommendations to win broad support. While there are critics everywhere, this is the closest we've come to doable action.

This would be a terrific start but why stop there? Let's use the momentum TO RETHINK HOW WE SEE THE WORLD—a big-picture longer-run strategy to build a sustainable America. That means fulfilling today's needs without compromising the needs of future generations. We need a culture of sustainability, finding technologies that use fewer resources per unit of production. We need vehicles that deliver far more miles per gallon. We need to stimulate innovations in clean, emission-free power sources. Were we to put a price on carbon, in a massive way businesses would jump into risk-taking and new investments. We need not just to improve appliances and change light bulbs, but begin to think in systems. For example, we need to design smart, sustainable cities—with energy-efficient buildings and factories, better use of infrastructure, land use with green belts and bike lanes and space for micro-wind turbines. Instead of subsidizing oil and coal, inspire efficient clean technologies.

A business colleague told me that a big bank with branches around the country was exploring ways to make every one of its buildings energy efficient. Think of the savings possible for heat and air conditioning, the new kinds of jobs needed, not to mention eco benefits.

Instead of Washington being a case study in dysfunction, it could become a launching pad for the next industrial revolution. With new designs promoting production efficiency, huge expenditures could be reduced across the board, with significant contributions to deficit reduction. Instead of a leadership vacuum in Wall Street focused on narrow thinking and greed, a new business culture of innovation would take over, and the momentum that in recent years migrated to Europe and China would return home. This in turn would lead to a whole new array of jobs. We know that in the old economy it was becoming evident that automation and globalization made it possible for America to produce all the goods and services required without its full labor force. Now, an entirely different generation of jobs will be needed for an increasingly green environment.

As we begin to think what the sustainable culture would look like, we'll need to raise the existing low average conservation IQ. Obviously, we're not just dealing with physical and economic and political problems—which will involve a shift in perception. We'll face a great learning challenge, to which our educational institutions have hardly begun to respond. There are immense opportunities for R & D, and innovation in curriculum and teacher training. As we re-examine our lifestyle and everyday habits to reduce waste, control excess consumption, choose eco-friendly products—think of the exciting challenges for the media and the arts as we cultivate new tastes and peer-group fashions.

There is expectation that our corporate capitalistic system would change. Currently, it is based on short-term profit, concentrating wealth that maintains huge income disparities, with minimum loyalty to workers or even the national welfare, or protecting the environment. The sustainability strategy can shift toward a more middle class-oriented capitalism. While the importance of profit and entrepreneurial innovation would remain, this model would respect the needs of workers who, after all, comprise most of the population. In America's earlier postwar years, the middle class was able to own a modest home, pay for health care and college, and retire with a manageable stipend. A sustainable economy would search for strategies that narrow the income gap and revitalize the middle class.

In conclusion, a sustainable America would significantly confront the deficit, joblessness, and ecological perils—worthy goals for 21st century America.

ODYSSEY
The Question of Jobs

by Belden Paulson

B.J. Everybody complains about job shortages but—as with the weather—nobody does anything about it. Well, make that nearly nobody. There are several local initiatives, and in this three-part series on "Joblessness: A Creative Response to one of America's Great, Long-term Challenges" Belden Paulson, political scientist and resident of Town Mitchell outlines the basic problem as well as two "tracks" towards a solution.

It is the basis for a talk presented Wednesday, May 15 for the World Future Society Milwaukee chapter. The first part summarizes the challenge. The next identifies short-term responses. The third takes a longer view of a "transformed" society.

B.P. Our economy can now produce all the goods and services our society needs without its total labor force. Modern technology has brought untold benefits in improving our level of living and reducing much of the most arduous tedium of work. But as our country's wealth dramatically increases while the number of workers needed to make that wealth significantly decreases, three central questions arise:

- With a sizable percentage of the population without a full-time job to support themselves and a family, how will they cover the basic necessities of life?

- With increased numbers of people jobless, what will they do with their free time? Would this be an opportunity to utilize their talents?

- If the people who invest the capital (the stockholders) and those who are still employed (workers and executives) take all or most of the wealth they produce, how will this accentuate the already rising economic inequality in America? For example, the top 1 percent have more wealth than the bottom 90 percent.

Keep in mind these background details:

- According to recent U.S. Bureau of Labor statistics (as of August 2012), 12.5 million people are unemployed; 2.6 million are the "forgotten unemployed" (unemployed for a year or more, some having given up any expectation of finding work); 8 million under-employed (working part-time). Total: 23.1 million. To be noted, there are 26.6 percent non-employed people ages 25-34, the highest in the industrial world.

- For companies to stay in business and compete globally, they must continually seek to increase their efficiency, adding automation devices that maximize productivity but require fewer workers.

- With technologies using computers and robots expected increasingly to take over the economy, we anticipate their use in many sectors. According to a recent issue of the *Future Policy Journal* they include: manufacturing (e.g. 3-D printers); health care (e.g. recent *Atlantic* issue on robots asking: Is your doctor becoming obsolete?); maintenance and domestic work (e.g. janitors, cleaners); professors (e.g. online courses); teachers (e.g. laptop computers); librarians (e.g. online book ordering); travel/rental car agencies (e.g. kiosks and online booking). The impact of these examples: more efficiency, fewer workers.

- Eminent social thinker Jeremy Rifkin in *The End of Work* concludes that this is only the beginning: World War II ended the 1930s depression and provided jobs; in the 1950s the National Defense Highway Act, and in the 1960s the Great Society war on poverty provided jobs. For forty postwar years as people moved from manufacturing into services, new jobs opened up. Electronics are now ushering in a new and different era. Norbert Weiner, father of cybernetics, predicted that the long-term consequences of automation technology will bring "the greatest unemployment we've ever seen." Management consultant Peter Drucker foresaw capitalism facing an unprecedented new issue: the looming disappearance of labor as a factor of production. Rifkin poses this question: Will the ever-mounting profits of expanding wealth be used for societal benefit, or for enriching the corporate world and thereby increasing the haves-have not gap?

Not to be overlooked is the impact of this new technology on the black population that migrated to northern cities after World War II. They filled unskilled and semiskilled jobs but automation has wiped out many of their jobs. Respected sociologist Julius Wilson argues in *When Work Disappears* that the key factor in today's inner city pathology has been joblessness. Conservative writer Charles Murray observes in his *Coming Apart*: "Our nation is coming apart at the seams—not ethnic seams but the seams of class."

In 1983 I helped to organize, through the University of Wisconsin, a national conference on "The Changing Role of Work." We assembled key leaders and thoughtful thinkers representing the best experience available—from business, unions, government, academia, to address the future of work—at that time with a less ominous future than today. Our two keynoters included path-breaking futurist Willis Harman. His seminal article in *The Futurist*, entitled "The Coming Transformation," concluded that modern industrial society, using the kind of data described above about joblessness, is facing fundamental challenges that will require nothing short of historic transformative shifts. The second keynoter was Richard Goodyear, vice president and legal counsel at Chrysler; the company had just received a government bailout to prevent bankruptcy. The company's CEO, Lee Iacocca, told us that we should invite Goodyear because he was responsible for the company's successful strategy. After the two talks, Goodyear whispered in my ear that Harman's transformation thesis was correct but he'd never say it publicly.

Jan brings desktop publishing expertise to High Wind; she goes into business with Louise in the dome she built in 1992

May 20, 2013

ODYSSEY
The Future of Work

by Belden Paulson

B.J. In this three-part series on "Joblessness: A Creative Response to one of America's Great, Long-term Challenges," Belden Paulson outlines two "tracks" towards a solution.

B.P. As mentioned last time, in 1983 I helped to organize a national conference through the University of Wisconsin on "The Changing Role of Work." We designed that conference around two tracks. Track One focused on the best ideas and practices for "what can be done here and now," assuming there is enlightened leadership that will focus on implementation. Track Two recognized that even the best of Track One will not be adequate. The long-run

crisis of joblessness is more fundamental. It is related to dilemmas facing the industrial system itself, and some sort of radical transformation is required. This conference was thirty years ago. The challenges we face today are more stark and real.

Keeping in mind the data we know about joblessness, let us envisage examples of Track One and Track Two strategies to confront today's likely trends.

A general Track One starting point is the need for an in-depth bipartisan national strategy that takes into account the short run and long run. The business community usually adds the great importance of reduced regulations and lower taxes to strengthen the economy and create jobs, although others note that much higher taxes in the postwar and Clinton years did not threaten near full employment.

Noteworthy Track One ideas include (in no particular order of importance):

- Critical importance of education and training; the unemployment rate of people age twenty-five and older with graduate and professional degrees is less than 4 percent, with those with B.A. degrees is less than 5 percent

- More effort is needed to develop skills to match available jobs (there are 3 million unfilled jobs)

- Bring back jobs from overseas (tax policy is important)

- Create incentives for hiring different categories of the non-employed

- Make investments in infrastructure-related jobs—also Depression-era WPA-type jobs

- Reduce high corporate compensation to provide money for more hiring and experimentation for new strategies

- Institute the thirty-hour workweek and job sharing (used some places in Europe)

- Make a massive revitalization effort in inner cities and depressed rural areas to upgrade skills and cultural level

The Track Two starting point recognizes that measures such as the above are valuable but insufficient. For example, Willis Harman in his "Coming Transformation" article writes: "The United States and other industrial nations now face a series of dilemmas that may be insoluble except by a sweeping transformation of their societies." These are: the growth dilemma ("We need continued economic growth but we cannot live with the consequences.") The control dilemma ("We need to guide technological innovation but we shun centralized control.") The distribution dilemma ("The industrialized nations find it costly to share the earth's resources with less developed nations, but a failure to do so might prove even more costly.") The work-roles dilemma ("Industrial society is increasingly unable to supply an adequate number of meaningful social roles").

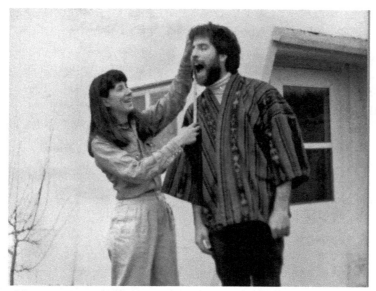

*Mary measures John for a new shirt in return for his figuring her taxes—
one of many barter transactions in the community*

May 22, 2013

ODYSSEY
Where Are All the Jobs Going?

by Belden Paulson

B.J. In this three-part series on joblessness, Belden Paulson outlines two "tracks" towards a solution.

Part One summarized the challenge. Part Two identified short-term responses. Part Three takes a longer view of a "transformed" society.

B.P. Keeping in mind the data we know about joblessness, let us envisage examples of Track One and Track Two strategies to confront today's likely trends.

A general Track One starting point is the need for an in-depth bipartisan national strategy that takes into account the short run and long run.

The Track Two starting point recognizes that short-term measures as such are valuable but insufficient. Noteworthy Track Two ideas and practices include:

- Guaranteed annual income as a matter of right to a minimal share in the production of society (no means test required). Proposed by economists Theobald and Heilbroner, and J. Robert Oppenheimer among others, but no action has been taken.

- Milton Friedman's "negative income tax" is the same idea of guaranteed income. He unsuccessfully proposed this to presidents Nixon and Reagan, given that he preferred a direct cash payment instead of bureaucratic welfare for the poor.

- "Third sector support" that utilizes more fully the voluntary world. Jeremy Rifkin proposes incentives and subsidies, including "social wages" and tax write-offs for voluntary work to utilize the vast pool of labor and talent for meeting community needs. Viewing a future where the market sector leaves vast joblessness, he asks: Will government use its resources "to finance additional police protection and build more jails to incarcerate a growing criminal class or finance alternative forms of work in the third sector?"

- Support "learning and development." Willis Harman in *Creative Work* notes that when production and consumption are no longer the main focus of one's life, then the "learning society," which includes self and community improvement, takes on added importance.

- Business itself becomes an agent of transformation. Harman is convinced that people in business, not in government, are society's real drivers. He identified numerous business leaders to establish the World Business Academy to invest their creative energy in helping to move toward a viable future.

- An example of transformation in business that combines the corporate and social worlds is the Mondragon complex in Spain. Established in the 1950s, there are 102 cooperatives employing over 100,000 people; it is the seventh largest business in Spain with annual revenue in the 6 billion euro range. Each cooperative donates 10 percent of yearly profits to education and social projects, and 10 percent to a social entrepreneur

pool for R & D. The highest paid workers earn no more than eight times the lowest paid workers, and despite the 20 percent unemployment and 50 percent among youth in Spain, Mondragon has no unemployment. This has happened through intelligent planning and voluntary reduction in work hours.

- Develop a sustainability policy that confronts the federal deficit, creates jobs, and focuses on ominous environmental perils. Two years ago President Obama established an eighteen-member bipartisan commission to figure out how to cut the deficit. Their recommendations included deficit reduction of $4 trillion by 2020 and numerous other ideas to cut spending and raise revenue. The Obama administration has not acted on this. Today a comprehensive environment-sensitive sustainability strategy is feasible. It would create new industries to increase energy efficiency in America's buildings and manufacturing and would provide a massive array of new jobs. At the same time costs incurred by government could be cut dramatically.

- Imaginative long-term thinking on our economic and cultural future is also needed. An example is found in Charles Eisenstein's *Sacred Economics* where the role of money itself is considered. The theme here is that money seems to be destroying the efficacy of many of our human social systems and the earth itself. The original purpose of money was to connect human gifts with human needs. Financiers have become masters of the universe, and new kinds of money are needed where gratitude and trust rather than money are what motivate peoples' actions.

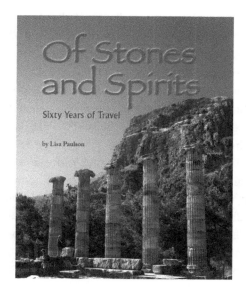

February 12, 2014

ODYSSEY
Local Authors Look State of the World in the Eye

by Barry Johanson

One of the most unique experiences I've had as a local publisher and printer was to come to work Monday and find two new books on my desk written by a couple with deep roots in Sheboygan County who had compiled 47 essays in recent years for *The Review*.

One, *Notes from the Field: Strategies toward Cultural Transformation*, is by Belden Paulson, a university political science professor and grassroots community organizer. The other, *Of Stones and Spirits, Sixty Years of Travel*, is by writer and artist Lisa Paulson who lived abroad and traveled widely with Belden (often with assorted family members) and kept detailed notes.

Currently, they divide their time between their solar home at High Wind in Town Mitchell and their mountain home in Vermont. The books were published by Thistlefield Books, Plymouth—www.thistlefieldbooks.com for ordering information.

This is not an attempt to review the books in depth. I have followed their writing in detail for many years, however, and in scanning these it is obvious each lives up to the summary statements on their covers, which follow here.

Notes from the Field

Today there are mini-revolutions in many parts of the world. It is not only the downtrodden who are rising up, but also the middle classes.

The institutions that are supposed to run things are not working very well. The challenges to solve the most critical problems seem beyond the capability of the governors.

Violence can spread to any area. Each circumstance is unique in its own setting, but behind all the eruptions, the essence is the same. PROBLEMS ARE NOT BEING SOLVED.

In the United States we still live in a fairly stable environment. But the protests we observe elsewhere are coming closer to home. Our government often appears incapable of confronting the great issues: environmental perils threatening the planet, growing economic and social inequality, inability to handle finances, chronic joblessness.

Despite the above, however, human creativity is really limitless. Go to any town or city, to any community, to find people at work who are defining the challenges and coming up with solutions. Sometimes they fail, but they are out there, and there are victories.

You have here a kind of casebook in problem solving, focusing on an array of issues. *Notes from the Field* pulls out key sections of materials compiled over many years—authentic, real-world experiences. The reader will find accumulated wisdom from decades of work. The overlapping themes are international, urban, community, and sustainable living. These flashes from frontline projects are all directed toward building a better world.

Of Stones and Spirits

Of Stones and Spirits is about freezing particular times and places in history—the poignant and delightful details that otherwise might have been lost. Lisa Paulson takes the reader on a magical carpet to places where she has worked and lived or visited over the past sixty years, from post-World War II ruins in Naples, Italy, to the much older ruins of Ephesus in Turkey—all juxtaposed against the lush backdrops of nature, which she delights in.

The travels begin with Lisa and her husband-to-be in 1953 and gradually expand over half a century to include children, grandchildren, and other relatives and colleagues. The book takes the reader inside the pages of meticulously kept notebooks where adventures were recorded in real time.

You will weep with her in the horrifying, heartbreaking wreckage of Naples, wonder with her at near-miraculous healings wrought by doctors of traditional medicine in China, and prowl with her through prehistoric caves in southwest France. You will drink wine on the terraces of restored, two-hundred-year-old farmhouses on sunlit Tuscan mountainsides and pound across Scottish sand dunes dotted with prickly golden gorse bushes to the North Sea....

And in countries with delicate, controversial, or changing governments and cultures, Lisa offers penetrating observations. She burrows beneath the pleasant surface attractions aimed at tourists, often because she is deliberately exposing herself to the raw crossroads that nations find themselves standing at in moments of seismic shifts and painful decisions.

AS YOU SEE IT
Impasse

by Lisa Paulson

To the Editor:

A sea of Bernie signs along all the country roads. This was Vermont where Bel and I were living this past summer and fall. Then, when we returned to rural Wisconsin in early November we were greeted by a sea of Trump signs in nearly every yard.

I grew up assuming that multiculturalism and global inclusiveness were the only natural and correct stances for thinking, sane, caring citizens. What happened in the recent election revealed that a huge swath of our country is not so sure; some may believe the opposite. And now, how do these vast, opposing constituencies, who "know" that theirs alone is the right, just way, expect to get along, to function together, make America work?

Clearly, an awful lot of Americans feel left out and ignored by those in power, and in the campaigns they found their respective champions. Interesting that many of the change-demanding Bernie and Trump folks hail from the same struggling economic and cultural sector—their fears and frustrations the same—an important clue as to how we might begin the conversation Could we listen, really hear each other out, discover if and where our basic values might mesh?

Bel points out that we're not for the status quo; we do need change. The liberal world order that emerged after World War II is being challenged now as never before. People are restless and angry, and authoritarian leadership with quick answers has appeal. How many remember that similar conditions prevailed in the 1930s in Europe, stoking the rise of fascism? The postwar institutions that emerged served for 70 years, but now they need radical upgrading to address today's urgent issues of race, poverty, and global warming.

Our Puritan forefathers, as well as all the other immigrants since then, came here with the burning dream of independence, of being able to express themselves freely and to better their situation. It's in our historical DNA to crave—insist on—personal autonomy. Even those of us who intentionally created communities of interdependence (as with our High Wind eco-experiment) found that in the end we also needed to honor our individual autonomy. We had to find ways to take into account the welfare of everyone, but without losing ourselves in the process. This past year great cadres of "little guys" rose up and spoke out, emboldened to defy and reject our creaky establishment machinery. They cheered the iconoclasts.

Our challenge may be to look at this next period as a unique opportunity to demonstrate our ingenuity and moral strength to break the impasse that grips us now.